DECEMBER 1996

Sunday	Monday	Tuesday	Wednesday	Thursday	Friday	Saturday
1	2	3	4	5	6	7
8	9	10	11	12	13	14
15	16	17	18	19	20	21
22	23	24 Christmas Eve	25 Christmas Day	26	27	28
29	30	31 New Year's Eve				

In the years to come, you'll be glad you noted the special times of the season on these pages.

Christmas
with Southern Living
1996

Oxmoor
House®

Christmas
with Southern Living
1996

Edited by Rebecca Brennan,
Julie Fisher, and Adrienne E. Short

©1996 by Oxmoor House, Inc.
Book Division of Southern Progress Corporation
P.O. Box 2463, Birmingham, Alabama 35201

Southern Living® is a federally registered trademark belonging to
Southern Living, Inc.

Library of Congress Catalog Card Number: 84-63032
ISBN: 0-8487-1509-8
ISSN: 0747-7791
Manufactured in the United States of America
First Printing 1996

Editor-in-Chief: Nancy Fitzpatrick Wyatt
Senior Homes Editor: Mary Kay Culpepper
Senior Foods Editor: Susan Carlisle Payne
Senior Editor, Editorial Services: Olivia Kindig Wells
Art Director: James Boone

Christmas with Southern Living 1996

Editor: Rebecca Brennan
Foods Editor: Julie Fisher
Assistant Editor: Adrienne E. Short
Assistant Art Director: Cynthia R. Cooper
Editorial Assistant: Cecile Y. Nierodzinski
Copy Editors: Keri Bradford Anderson, L. Amanda Owens
Senior Photographers: Jim Bathie, John O'Hagan
Senior Photo Stylists: Kay E. Clarke, Katie Stoddard
Director, Test Kitchens: Kathleen Royal Phillips
Assistant Director, Test Kitchens: Gayle Hays Sadler
Test Kitchens Home Economists: Susan Hall Bellows,
    Julie Christopher, Michele Brown Fuller, Natalie E. King,
    Elizabeth Tyler Luckett, Iris Crawley O'Brien,
    Jan A. Smith
Illustrator: Kelly Davis
Production and Distribution Director: Phillip Lee
Associate Production Managers: Theresa L. Beste,
    Vanessa D. Cobbs
Production Coordinator: Marianne Jordan Wilson
Production Assistant: Valerie L. Heard

Front cover: German Chocolate Truffles, page 52;
    Keepsake Boxes, page 108.
Back cover, top left: Oak Leaf Wreath, page 72; top right:
    Golden Angel Ornament, page 64; bottom: Velvet and
    Organza Stocking, page 56.

CONTENTS

6 Country Inn Christmas

22 The Christmas Tree

32 The Holiday Table

42 A Taste of Christmas

48 Coffee Charms

54 Decorations

76 Sweets in Seconds

86 Tasteful Centerpieces

94 Christmas Presents

106 Gift Wrappings

116 Gifts from the Kitchen

124 Nutty Desserts

134 Christmas Dinner

144 Patterns
154 Sources
156 Index
160 Contributors

COUNTRY INN CHRISTMAS

Donna Hamilton, host of The Learning Channel's "Great Country Inns," chooses three of her favorite Southern inns. We share them, decorated for Christmas, with you.

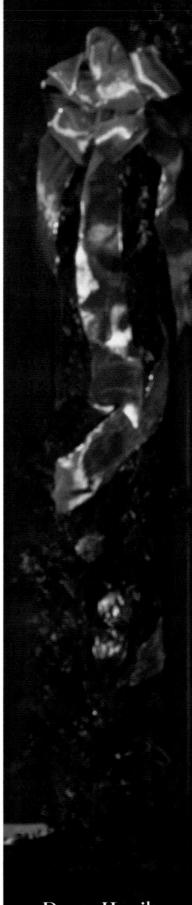

Donna Hamilton visits The Inn at Blackberry Farm.

6

The Inn at Blackberry Farm

"Even on the chilliest day," says Donna, "there's a sunny country welcome here."

Four English country-style houses make up this 1,100-acre pastoral estate that is nestled in the Great Smoky Mountains of Tennessee. An icy pond and quaint split-rail fence set an idyllic scene for a charming holiday retreat.

You'll know this gourmet getaway by the friendly staff. They go out of their way to provide a "sweet service that is rare to find," Donna says.

Just inside the main house, you'll find luxurious boxwood garlands framing the doorways that lead you through the house (shown at right). The garlands are adorned with pinecones, pomegranates, gold ribbon, gilded baby artichokes, ornamental angels, roses, and hydrangea. The entire inn is filled with decorating ideas that will inspire holiday trimmings in your own home.

Hundreds of dried miniature spray roses, the inn's
signature flowers, frame the fireplace and adorn
a gold-themed Christmas tree.

Settle onto a cozy sofa in the living room, and relax with a glowing fire crackling at your feet. Every table is set with creative ideas—like the bowl brimming with orange pomanders that have been dusted with cinnamon and studded with cloves.

The main house veranda (seen through the window of the dining room, above) boasts the "best seat and scene" in the house, with a long terrace lined with white rockers for viewing nature's finest artwork.

You won't leave without catching Blackberry Farm's contagious Christmas spirit. During the holidays, every window displays a wreath—over 150 of them! Local high school carolers will draw you to the piano after dinner. And you'll receive a stocking with a personalized ornament and other goodies when you come for breakfast on Christmas morning.

CHRISTMAS IS ONE OF TWO TIMES YEARLY that Chef John Fleer serves a harvest buffet. As if in his own home, he presides at the head of the table, ready to greet you with the virtues of his smoked cured ham and grits-and-smoked oyster casserole.

Chef Fleer enjoys a reputation for refined "Foothills Cuisine"—new American cooking that reflects his regional heritage. His comforting style promotes cornmeal, ham hocks, grits and greens, country ham, and stack pies. And he polishes it all to his discriminating Southern palate. Here, he shares one of his favorite breakfast recipes.

Chef Fleer offers a cookie to Donna Hamilton. In his kitchen, guests are welcome any time.

Sally Lunn French Toast

Three toppings, grilled figs, and Tennessee bacon make this buttery French toast worth rising for on Christmas morning.

    ¼ cup dried cherries or currants
    ¼ cup apple cider
    1 tablespoon bourbon (optional)
    1 medium orange
    1 cup milk
    ½ cup butter
      Pinch of saffron
    1 package active dry yeast
    ¼ cup warm water (105° to 115°)
  4¾ cups all-purpose flour
    1 tablespoon salt
    ¼ cup firmly packed brown sugar
    3 large eggs, lightly beaten
      French Toast Custard
      Warm Winter Fruits
      Honey-Pecan Butter
      Cinnamon-Maple Syrup

Combine cherries, apple cider, and bourbon; let stand 30 minutes.

Working over a small bowl to catch juice, remove rind from orange, using a sharp paring knife or vegetable peeler. Cut pith away from rind. Finely chop rind. Squeeze juice from orange. Combine juice, chopped rind, 1 cup milk, ½ cup butter, and saffron in a saucepan; heat until butter melts, stirring occasionally. Cool to 120° to 130°.

Combine yeast and warm water in a 1-cup liquid measuring cup; let stand 5 minutes.

Combine flour, salt, and brown sugar in a large mixing bowl. Combine milk mixture, yeast mixture, and 3 eggs; stir well. Gradually add liquid mixture to flour mixture, beating at high speed of an electric mixer. Beat 2 additional minutes at medium speed. Stir in cherries and liquid.

Cover and let rise in a warm place (85°), free from drafts, 45 minutes or until doubled in bulk. Stir batter well.

Spoon batter into a well-greased 9" x 5" x 3" loaf-pan. Cover and let rise in a warm place, free from drafts, 30 minutes or until almost doubled in bulk.

Bake at 400° for 15 minutes. Reduce heat to 350°, and bake 20 additional minutes. Cool in pan 10

Sally Lunn French Toast

Warm Winter Fruits

This fruit mixture also makes a great strudel filling.

 2 medium-size Granny Smith apples, peeled and
    diced
 1 firm ripe pear, peeled and diced
 2 tablespoons brown sugar
 2 tablespoons finely chopped dried cherries
 1 tablespoon plus 1 teaspoon finely chopped
    orange rind
 1 tablespoon finely chopped lemon rind
 1 tablespoon finely chopped dried apricots
 1 tablespoon currants
 ½ teaspoon ground cardamom
    Pinch of freshly grated nutmeg
 1 cup apple cider
 1 tablespoon applejack (optional)
 2 teaspoons fresh lemon juice

Combine all ingredients in large saucepan; stir well. Bring to a boil; reduce heat, and simmer, uncovered, 15 minutes or until apple and pear are tender, stirring often. **Yield:** 2¼ cups.

Honey-Pecan Butter
 ½ cup butter
 1½ tablespoons honey
 2 tablespoons pecan pieces, toasted

Combine butter and honey in a small mixing bowl; beat at low speed of an electric mixer 1 minute or until creamy. Stir in pecan pieces. **Yield:** ⅔ cup.

Cinnamon-Maple Syrup

Store-bought maple syrup remains a good choice if you're in a pinch for time.

 ½ cup firmly packed brown sugar
 ¼ cup sugar
 1 cup maple syrup
 ¼ cup water
 2 tablespoons light corn syrup
 1 (3") stick cinnamon
 2 whole allspice

Combine all ingredients in a small saucepan; stir well. Bring to a boil; reduce heat, and simmer, uncovered, 15 minutes. **Yield:** 1½ cups.

minutes. Remove bread from pan, and cool completely on a wire rack.

Cut loaf crosswise into 8 slices. Cut each slice in half diagonally. Dip each bread slice into French Toast Custard, coating well.

Arrange 8 half-slices of bread on a preheated greased griddle, and cook 3 minutes on each side or until browned. Repeat procedure with remaining bread slices, regreasing griddle, if needed.

Cut a slit in top of each piece of French toast within ½" of edge. Stuff each pocket with 2 tablespoons Warm Winter Fruits. Serve French toast with Honey-Pecan Butter, Cinnamon-Maple Syrup, and additional Warm Winter Fruits mixture. **Yield:** 8 servings.

French Toast Custard
 ¼ cup sifted powdered sugar
 ½ teaspoon ground cinnamon
    Pinch of freshly grated nutmeg
 1½ cups milk
 4 large eggs, lightly beaten
 2 tablespoons dark rum (optional)
 1 tablespoon vanilla extract

Combine all ingredients in a shallow bowl; stir well with a wire whisk. **Yield:** 2 cups.

The Inn at Perry Cabin

THIS INN PROVES THERE'LL ALWAYS BE an England—even if it's on this side of the Atlantic. Climb the garland-wrapped staircase, and you'll be tempted to imagine that you're staying in a genteel English manor house. Even the blanket of snow is the color of Devonshire cream.

This little bit of Britain is situated on the shores of Fogg Cove just outside the historic town of St. Michaels, Maryland. Sir Bernard Ashley, widower of Laura Ashley and head of the family's furnishings empire, owns the inn. As you might expect, Ashley fabrics and wallpapers grace the rooms, as seen in the inn's dining room shown here.

IN THE SITTING ROOM, YOU'LL FEEL cosseted when you sink into a down-filled chair in a place tastefully bedecked for the holidays (left). You'll want to rise, though, for teatime, when Chef Mark Saiter bakes meltingly delicious Scones and serves them with his addicting Raspberry Preserves. His recipes follow.

Scones

These flaky blonde biscuits keep with Olde English tradition.

3½ cups all-purpose flour
2¼ teaspoons baking powder
 ¼ cup sugar
  1 cup butter
 ½ cup golden raisins
 ⅔ cup milk
  1 large egg
  1 tablespoon milk
  2 teaspoons sugar
    Raspberry Preserves
    Whipping cream, lightly whipped

Combine first 3 ingredients in a large bowl; cut in butter with a pastry blender until mixture is crumbly. Stir in raisins. Combine ⅔ cup milk and egg, stirring with a wire whisk. Gradually add milk mixture to flour mixture, stirring with a fork just until dry ingredients are moistened. Turn dough out onto a lightly floured surface, and knead 4 times.

  Roll or pat dough to 1" thickness; cut with a 2" biscuit cutter. Place dough cutouts on a lightly greased baking sheet. Brush with 1 tablespoon milk, and sprinkle with 2 teaspoons sugar.

  Bake at 350° for 15 minutes or until barely golden. Let cool slightly on a wire rack. Serve warm with Raspberry Preserves and whipped cream.
Yield: 1½ dozen.

**Scones with
Raspberry Preserves**

Raspberry Preserves
  2 pounds fresh or frozen raspberries
  1 cup black currants
  2 tablespoons lemon juice
  5 cups sugar

Combine first 3 ingredients in a large stainless steel Dutch oven. Bring to a boil; cook 5 minutes, stirring occasionally. Add sugar; bring to a boil. Cook over medium heat until a candy thermometer registers 220°, stirring occasionally. Remove from heat; cool completely. Pour preserves into airtight containers; store in refrigerator. **Yield:** 5 half pints.

Dairy Hollow House

YOU'LL FIND ARKANSAS WARMTH AND hospitality from the moment you arrive at this place that's "the very slice of Eureka Springs," according to Crescent Dragonwagon, owner and chef.

Two things magnify the joys of the Christmas season at the oldest inn in the Ozarks. One is literally a *signature* holiday tablecloth; the other is a lavish dessert array atop it. The heirloom tablecloth has evolved from a simple table runner into the inn's holiday guest register of sorts. Since 1984, the tablecloth has served as a historical record of over 100 friends and family members who have marked their presence in pen.

As for the desserts that crown the cloth (at right), Crescent may alter the recipe lineup slightly each year, but her Browned Butter Pecan Pie holds a reserved seat at the table. Find this recipe and a make-ahead breakfast casserole on the next pages. Both highlight Crescent's "Nouveau Z'arks Cuisine"—a fresh take on regional Ozarks flavors.

Crescent and husband Ned Shank remember friends fondly and stitch over each signature with bright threads, as if to ingrain the memories deeper.

Crescent's Overnight
Cornbread Strata

Crescent's Overnight Cornbread Strata

Unpack Crescent's famed breakfast in a basket to discover this egg casserole, shown at left.

Skillet-Sizzled Buttermilk Cornbread, cooled
  and crumbled into large pieces
Vegetable cooking spray
1½ cups (6 ounces) shredded sharp Cheddar
  cheese
¾ cup diced cooked ham
8 large eggs, lightly beaten
2 cups milk
¼ teaspoon salt
⅛ teaspoon freshly ground pepper
Pinch of dried dillweed
Pinch of dried basil
Dash of hot sauce
Dash of Worcestershire sauce

Place crumbled cornbread in a 15" x 10" x 1" jelly-roll pan. Bake at 325° for 20 minutes, stirring after 10 minutes. Let cool.

Place cornbread pieces in a 13" x 9" x 2" baking dish coated with cooking spray. Layer cheese over cornbread; sprinkle ham over cheese.

Combine eggs and remaining 7 ingredients; stir well. Pour over cornbread mixture. Cover and chill overnight.

Bake, uncovered, at 350° for 45 minutes or until set and golden. Let stand 10 minutes before serving. **Yield:** 8 servings.

Skillet-Sizzled Buttermilk Cornbread

1 cup whole grain yellow cornmeal
1 cup unbleached all-purpose flour
1 tablespoon baking powder
½ teaspoon salt
¼ teaspoon baking soda
1¼ cups whole buttermilk
1 large egg, lightly beaten
2 tablespoons sugar
¼ cup vegetable oil
2 tablespoons butter
Vegetable cooking spray

Combine first 4 ingredients in a large bowl; make a well in center of mixture.

Stir soda into buttermilk. Combine buttermilk mixture, egg, sugar, and oil; add to dry ingredients, stirring just until moistened. Place butter in a 9" or 10" cast-iron skillet coated with cooking spray. Place over medium-high heat until butter melts. Pour batter into prepared skillet. Bake at 375° for 25 to 30 minutes or until golden. **Yield:** 8 servings.

Browned Butter Pecan Pie

This is Crescent's most sought after dessert.

½ cup butter
¾ cup light corn syrup
¼ cup honey
1 cup sugar
1 teaspoon vanilla extract
⅛ teaspoon salt
3 large eggs, lightly beaten
1 cup chopped pecans
1 unbaked (9") pastry shell
Whipped cream

Cook butter in a small saucepan over medium-low heat 6 to 8 minutes or until browned. (Do not stir.) Remove from heat, and set aside.

Combine corn syrup and next 5 ingredients; stir well with a wire whisk. Stir in browned butter and pecans. Pour mixture into pastry shell.

Bake at 425° for 10 minutes. Reduce oven temperature to 325°, and bake 40 to 45 additional minutes or until center of pie is almost set. (Cover pie with aluminum foil to prevent excessive browning after 25 minutes, if necessary.) Cool completely on a wire rack. (Pie will become firm as it cools.) Serve with whipped cream. **Yield:** one 9" pie.

For more information about these country inns, see Sources on page 154.

THE CHRISTMAS TREE

Greet your guests with this innovative decoration that spans the holidays. We show you three easy variations on the next pages. Also in this chapter: A velvet skirt and a ribbon-wrapped topper are the ticket for a tree with updated style. And for sparkle, we feature glistening ornaments made from wire and beads.

A Tree for All Seasons

A Tree for All Seasons

WITH JUST A FEW CHANGES, YOUR entryway will be appropriately dressed for the holidays from Thanksgiving through New Year's Day.

You will need: (for all 3 trees)
Styrofoam cone to fit urn
fresh ivy leaves
hot-glue gun and glue sticks
spray acrylic sealer
Styrofoam sheets
urn or outdoor planter
florist's picks
wire

For Harvest Tree:
artificial fruit and vegetables: grapes, miniature
    pumpkins, gourds
artificial or natural dried leaves
grapevine

For Christmas Tree:
fresh greenery
ornaments: glass, jumbo plastic

For New Year's Tree:
Mylar sheets: gold, magenta, purple, yellow
New Year's party favors
large Styrofoam stars
gold spray paint
Mylar star wire garland: gold, purple

Note: For cone, see Sources on page 154.

1. For tree cone and base, using hot glue, cover cone with ivy leaves. Let dry. For glossy finish, spray ivy-covered cone with acrylic sealer. Let dry. From Styrofoam sheet, cut out circle to fit over urn opening

Harvest Tree

(see photo). With dab of hot glue, glue Styrofoam circle to bottom of cone. Let dry. (*Note:* Replace circle before making each type of tree. Circle will pop off of cone bottom.) Set cone with circle over urn opening. If necessary, to steady urn, place brick or heavy object inside urn.

2. For Harvest Tree, hot-glue each artificial fruit and vegetable to end of florist's pick. Let dry. For grapes, wrap grape stem and florist's pick together with wire. To attach fruit and vegetables around base of cone, insert ends of florist's picks into Styrofoam circle (see photo). End of picks will stick through circle into urn. Using wire, wrap bunches

Christmas Tree

New Year's Tree

of leaves to florist's picks. Insert leaves into circle, filling spaces between fruit and vegetables. Insert grapevine ends into circle, allowing some vine pieces to dangle below fruit and vegetables (see photo).

3. For Christmas Tree, insert greenery stems into circle around tree base as in Step 2. If necessary to secure, wire bunches of greenery to florist's picks. Hot-glue each ornament to florist's pick. Let dry. Insert ornaments into circle, filling spaces between greenery (see photo).

4. For New Year's Tree, bunch up sheets of Mylar. Using wire, wrap Mylar bunches to florist's picks. Using wire, wrap party favors to florist's picks. Insert Mylar bunches and party favors into circle around base of cone as in Step 2 (see photo). Spray Styrofoam stars with gold paint. Let dry. Insert 1 end of florist's pick into each star and stick stars into circle (see photo). Wind Mylar star garlands around cone (see photo). Secure ends of garland to cone with dab of hot glue.

Velvet Tree Skirt

A circle of jester points and jingle bells surrounds the tree with elfish charm.

You will need:
pattern and diagram on page 153
4 yards 45"-wide dark green velvet
pushpin
1¼ yards string
dressmaker's pen
4 yards lining fabric
4 yards 45"-wide light green velvet
2 hooks and eyes
transparent thread
29 large jingle bells

Note: All seam allowances are ½". Finished skirt is 74" in diameter. For velvet, see Sources on page 154.

1. To make skirt, cut dark green velvet into 2 (2-yard) pieces. With right sides facing and raw edges aligned, stitch pieces together along 1 long edge, making sure nap runs in same direction. Repeat with lining fabric. Referring to diagram on page 153, fold seamed velvet piece in half and then in half again. To mark outer circle, tie push-pin to 1 end of string. Stick pushpin through folded corner of velvet. Measure and mark 36" of string. Tie loose end of string to dressmaker's pen at this point to make compass. Holding string taut, draw arc with 36" radius on velvet. To mark inner circle, draw arc with 1½" radius in same

manner. Cut out circles through all layers. Open skirt and cut straight line from outer edge to inner circle for opening. Repeat with lining fabric.

2. To make points, with right sides together, fold light green velvet along bias. Using pattern on page 153, with dressmaker's pen, transfer pattern to velvet once; flip pattern where indicated and trace again. Continue flipping and tracing pattern to make continuous row of points to within 1½" of fabric edge. Move pattern to new area of velvet and repeat as necessary to trace total of 29 points. With right sides facing and raw edges aligned, stitch corresponding strips of points together. For each strip, clip points, trim seams, and turn. Press flat.

3. To assemble, lay velvet piece right side up on flat surface. With raw edges aligned, pin point strips to right side of skirt around outside edge, overlapping strips slightly where they meet. Baste in place and then remove pins. With right sides facing, raw edges aligned, and points toward center, stitch velvet and lining pieces together, leaving 8" opening in 1 straight edge of skirt. Clip curves and turn. Slipstitch opening closed. Press.

4. To finish, on lining side of skirt opening, stitch 1 hook each 2" and 7" from inner circle along 1 straight edge. Repeat to stitch eyes on opposite side of opening. Using transparent thread, stitch 1 jingle bell to end of each point.

Wire & Bead Ornaments

Dangle these dainties near a window to catch
the bright winter sun.

You will need:
wire clippers
**24- or 32-gauge steel wire (Size will depend on
   sizes of bead holes.)**
beads in assorted colors and sizes
pliers
ribbon or trim for hanger

Note: For beads, you can unstring costume jewelry.
For purchased beads, see Sources on page 154.

1. To make each ornament, cut 1 length of wire to
desired size plus 8". Cut second piece of wire ½"
shorter. Set shorter length aside.

Thread beads onto longer wire, leaving 4" of wire
free at both ends. Bend wire into desired shape. Twist
ends together. In same manner, thread beads onto
shorter wire, bend, and twist ends together.

2. To assemble, place smaller shape sideways into
larger shape. Twist wire ends of both shapes together.
Slide large bead onto twisted wires. With pliers,
shape twisted wires into loop. Push wire ends into
large bead hole, forming ring.

3. To hang ornament, thread ribbon or trim
through wire ring. Knot to form hanger.

For the star and the garland at right, follow the general directions with this variation: Bend wire into a star shape and thread with assorted beads, either filling the wire shape with beads or spacing a few as shown. Then attach a length of wire to the star. String assorted beads onto this length. Put the combination on the tree or use the star alone as a package topper.

Gold-Ribbon Tree Topper

This mossy sphere will crown your tree with glory.
Smaller Styrofoam balls wrapped with moss and ribbon
and then hung on the tree would make a
pretty complement.

You will need:
8"-diameter Styrofoam ball
melon baller
thick craft glue
2 bags green moss
plastic knife
3 yards ⅜"-wide antique gold braid
T-pins
5½ yards gold twisted cord
24 to 48 upholstery nails
1½ yards 1"-wide gold mesh wire-edged ribbon
3 yards 1½"-wide gold sheer wire-edged ribbon
6 yards 1½"-wide gold and sheer plaid wire-edged
    ribbon
1½ yards ⅝"-wide gold-and-black striped wire-
    edged ribbon
S-head craft pins

Note: If desired, rest ball on widemouthed quart jar
while working. For Styrofoam ball and ribbon, see
Sources on page 154.

1. To make base, using melon baller, make
3"-deep opening in ball.

2. To cover ball with moss, shake moss to
remove debris. (*Note:* Mist moss with water for
easier handling.) Tear moss into approximately
4" patches. Using plastic knife, spread glue onto
ball. Cover surface with moss, alternating patches of
light and dark moss.

3. To wrap with braid, beginning at base of ball,
wrap ball with braid, tucking raw end of braid into
opening in base. Use T-pins to temporarily hold
braid in place. Wrap ball with 4 yards of twisted

cord in same manner. To secure areas where cord
and braid cross, push T-pins firmly into ball. Then
insert upholstery nail beside each pin, concealing
pin. Place nails where desired; not all intersections
need to be decorated. Remove extra T-pins.
(*Note:* Apply glue to back of each nail, if necessary,
to hold in place.)

4. To add ribbon, from mesh ribbon, cut
3 (18") lengths, trimming ribbon ends at an angle.
Stack mesh lengths and set aside. From plain sheer
ribbon, cut 6 (18") lengths, cutting V in ribbon ends.
Stack 3 lengths on top of mesh lengths.
    Place center of stacked ribbon lengths on
center top of moss-covered ball and secure, using
craft pin. Tie remaining plain sheer lengths to 1 craft
pin each. Pin ribbons at base of ball, spacing evenly
around opening.
    From plaid sheer ribbon, cut 6 (18") lengths and
3 (36") lengths, cutting V in ribbon ends. Fold 3
(18") lengths into loops for bow. Center remaining
18" lengths on top of loops. Secure to center top of
moss ball on top of mesh and plain sheer ribbons,
using craft pin.
    Tie 36" lengths to 1 craft pin each. Pin ribbons at
base of ball between plain sheer ribbons.
    From striped ribbon, cut 3 (18") lengths, trimming
ribbon ends at an angle. Stack lengths and set aside.
From remaining twisted cord, cut 3 (18") lengths.
Stack lengths and tie to craft pin. Use this pin to
secure striped ribbon lengths to top of moss-covered
ball in center of other ribbons. Wrap striped ribbon
around pencil to make tight spirals.

5. To place on tree, position opening in base of
tree topper on top of tree and press down firmly.

THE HOLIDAY TABLE

Rose-kissed velvet topiaries are a romantic table topper; we tell you how to make them on the next page. There are also instructions for easy-to-make organdy place mats that are crisply formal. For your casual gatherings, the simple motifs of hand-painted tableware are as welcome as your guests.

Velvet Topiaries

Velvet Topiaries

RIBBON ROSES BLOOM ON THESE PLUSH trees. Use one for a romantic accent or group them for a dramatic arrangement at the center of the table.

You will need (for 1 topiary):
Styrofoam ball
string
straight pins
tissue paper
velvet
craft glue
velvet cording
ribbon roses
hot-glue gun with glue sticks
florist's foam
terra-cotta pot or decorative container
stick
Spanish moss
craft knife
ribbon for bow

Note: Velvet and cording amounts will vary depending on size of Styrofoam ball used. For Styrofoam ball, see Sources on page 154.

1. For topiary top, cut 2 pieces of string equal in length to circumference of ball. To make pattern for cutting velvet, cross 2 pieces of string around ball, dividing ball into quarters. Use pins to secure strings at crossing points on top and bottom of ball. Trace outline of 1 quarter section onto tissue paper. Cut out pattern. Using pattern, cut 4 quarter pieces from velvet. Using craft glue, glue velvet pieces onto ball, matching seams. Let dry.

2. For velvet cording, measure along 1 seam from bottom, over top, and to bottom of ball. Cut 2 pieces of velvet cording to this measurement, less ½" to allow space at bottom for attaching ball to base. Using hot glue, glue cording pieces over quarter piece seams, starting ¼" from bottom point and crossing pieces at top. Let dry. Using hot glue, glue ribbon roses to top and sides of ball (see photo).

3. For topiary base, cut florist's foam into pieces to fit inside pot. Fill pot to rim with foam, using craft glue to secure foam to bottom of pot. Let dry. Dab craft glue on 1 end of stick. Push stick down into center of foam until end reaches bottom of pot. Using craft glue, cover foam surface with moss.

4. To attach ball to base, use craft knife to make small hole at bottom point of ball. Dab craft glue on end of stick. Place stick into hole and push until stick reaches middle of ball. Tie ribbon bow under ball. Secure bow to stick with dab of hot glue.

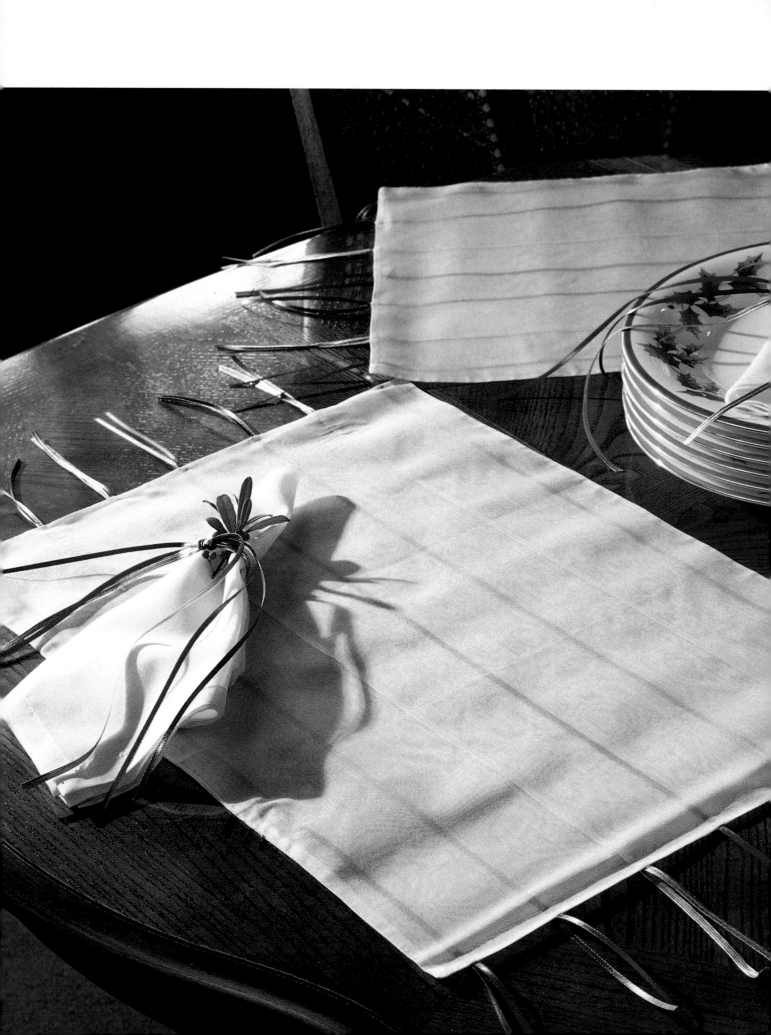

Ribbon-Striped Place Mats

ONCE YOU'VE MADE THE MATS, TIE extra lengths of ribbon around napkins and tuck bits of greenery into the bows.

You will need (for 4 place mats):
4 yards 54"-wide white silk organdy
19 yards ⅛"-wide red satin ribbon
12½ yards ⅛"-wide green satin ribbon
12½ yards ⅛"-wide gold braid

Note: Finished place mat size is 14" x 20". All seam allowances are ¼".

1. **To cut out each place mat,** from organdy, cut 2 (14½" x 20½") rectangles. From ribbon, cut 6 (28") lengths from red and 4 (28") lengths from green. From gold braid, cut 4 (28") lengths.

2. **To sew place mat,** on wrong side of 1 organdy rectangle, baste alternating colors of ribbons in place (see photo). Begin with red ribbon 1" from top of rectangle, space ribbons approximately 2" apart, and leave 4" free on each side for trim. With right sides together and raw edges aligned, stitch 2 organdy rectangles together, leaving opening for turning. Remove basting stitches. Clip corners, trim seams, and turn. Machine-stitch opening closed. Press. Repeat for remaining place mats.

Jeweled Candle Collars

THESE PETALS DRESS YOUR TAPERS WITH pretty pendants. And they're practical, too: They keep wax off the tabletop.

You will need:
patterns on page 153
cardboard and heavy paper for patterns
36-gauge brass or copper foil: 4½" square for
    small collar, 5½" square for large collar
5½" square soft wood
awl
inexpensive sewing scissors with 2" blades
knitting needle (or other blunt-pointed tool)
¾"-diameter dowel
brass jewelry pins
assorted glass beads
needle-nose pliers
20-gauge brass wire
wire cutters

Note: For foil, see Sources on page 154.

Candle collar before shaping petals.

1. To make pattern, using patterns on page 153, trace cutting pattern onto cardboard and tooling pattern onto heavy paper. Cut out patterns. Transfer outline of cutting pattern onto foil square.

2. To cut out collar, protect work surface with wood scrap. Place cutting pattern over metal square. For pendant-attachment holes, use awl to pierce through pattern and metal where indicated by circles on tips of petals on pattern. Punch hole at center of pattern where indicated by circle.

Using less pressure (in order to dent and not to pierce metal), make indentations at base of petals and at center where indicated by circles. Remove pattern. Carefully cut out collar with scissors. Cut each petal from tip to base.

3. To make tooling pattern on petals, place cutout collar on thick layer of newspaper to protect work surface. Position tooling pattern on top of 1 petal. With knitting needle, gently transfer tooling pattern. Remove pattern and retrace lines to deepen indentations. Repeat with remaining petals.

4. To open center and create prongs for slipping collar on candle holder, make 8 small cuts from center of shape to adjacent indentations on metal (see pattern). Push prongs apart. Insert dowel through hole to shape opening. Gently bend large petals up and small petals down to create a flower-like effect.

5. To make plain beaded pendant, thread approximately 2" of assorted beads onto jewelry pin, leaving about ½" of wire free at top. Bend wire with pliers to form small hook. Insert hook into hole at tip of 1 small petal on collar. Close hook with pliers to secure. Repeat to make another plain bead pendant. Attach to opposite small petal.

To make pendant with wire shape at top, thread 1½" of assorted beads onto jewelry pin. Cut off ½" of wire at top of pin. Form remaining wire into closed circle. Cut 6" length of brass wire. Form small hook at 1 end of wire. Shape remaining wire into coil, spiral, or zigzag shape. Form small hook at bottom of wire shape. Insert hook into top of beaded wire and close to secure. Form small hook at top of shaped wire. Attach as for plain pendant to remaining small petals.

Tree & Holly Tableware

HAND-PAINTED PLATES, NAPKINS, AND A tablecloth are just a stencil away. The border is a cinch to paint freehand–variations only add homespun charm.

Stenciled Charger
You will need:
pattern and diagram on page 145
unfinished wooden plate
wood sealer
clear peel-and-stick vinyl shelf covering
paintbrushes: ½" stencil, #1 flat, ¾" flat, #6 flat
acrylic paints: leaf green, crimson, cherry red
gold gloss metallic paint
gloss varnish

Note: For plate, paints, and paintbrushes, see Sources on page 154.

1. **To prepare plate,** apply 1 coat of wood sealer, following manufacturer's directions.

2. **To make tree stencil,** cut piece of vinyl covering to fit inner circle of plate. Trace tree stencil pattern onto paper side of vinyl circle. Cut out tree from vinyl, without cutting from outside edge to center. Peel paper backing from circle and press vinyl stencil onto center of plate.
   Using stencil brush and green paint, stencil tree onto center of plate. Let dry. Using stencil brush and gold paint, lightly and randomly dab over tree (see photo). Let dry. Carefully remove stencil.

3. **To paint rim,** using #1 flat brush and crimson paint, paint squiggly line along inner edge of plate rim (see photo). Let dry.
   Using ¾" flat brush and crimson paint, paint points along outer edge of plate rim (see photo and diagram). Let dry. Using tip of handle and gold paint, apply 1 dot inside each point. Let dry.

Using #6 flat brush and green paint, paint evenly spaced squiggles around plate rim (see photo). Using tip of handle and red paint, apply 3 dots for holly berries between each squiggle. Let dry.

4. To protect painted charger, apply several thin layers of gloss varnish, letting dry between coats. To use, place clear glass plate on top of painted charger.

Stenciled Tablecloth

You will need:
pattern on page 145
white tablecloth
clear peel-and-stick vinyl shelf covering
paintbrushes: ½" stencil, #10 shader, #6 flat
fabric painting medium
acrylic paints: leaf green, cherry red
gold gloss metallic paint

Note: Wash, dry, and press tablecloth before painting. For best results, do not use fabric softener.

1. For placement of tree stencils, fold tablecloth in half and then in half again to locate center. Make crease along folds to mark. Unfold cloth. Cut piece of paper into 8"-diameter circle. To determine center, fold paper circle in half, in half again, and then in half again. Unfold paper and mark 8 evenly spaced points around outer edge of circle at creases. Place center of paper circle in center of tablecloth; pin. Using pencil, lightly mark tablecloth at points on paper circle. Remove paper circle.

2. To stencil trees, using pattern, trace tree stencil onto paper side of vinyl covering 8 times, leaving at least 3½" between each tree. Cut trees apart, leaving about 1½" around each tree. Cut out trees from stencils, without cutting from outside edge to center. Working with 1 stencil at a time, gently peel paper backing from vinyl. Place stencil, sticky side down, on tablecloth, aligning top of tree with 1 pencil mark. Continue in this manner to place remaining tree stencils in circle.
Add fabric painting medium to acrylic paints, following manufacturer's directions. Using stencil brush and green paint, stencil each tree. Let dry. Using stencil brush and gold metallic paint, lightly

and randomly dab over tree (see photo). Let dry. Carefully remove stencil.

3. To paint freehand holly border, using shader brush and green paint, paint squiggles below base of each tree (see photo). Using tip of handle and red paint, apply 3 dots for holly berries between each squiggle. Using flat brush, repeat squiggle and dot design around border.

4. Before using cloth, let painted areas dry at least 24 hours. Then heat-set by covering with soft cloth and pressing with hot iron.

Stenciled Napkin

You will need:
white napkin
#10 shader paintbrush
fabric painting medium
acrylic paints: leaf green, cherry red

Note: Wash, dry, and press napkin before painting. For best results, do not use fabric softener.

1. To paint freehand holly border, add fabric painting medium to acrylic paints, following manufacturer's directions. Using shader brush and green paint, paint evenly spaced squiggles around border (see photo). Using tip of handle and red paint, apply 3 dots for holly berries between each squiggle.

2. Before using napkin, let painted areas dry at least 24 hours. Then heat-set by covering with soft cloth and pressing with hot iron.

Carol Tipton of Calera, Alabama, recalls the annual "unveiling" of her grandmother's Lane cake on the table, set for Christmas Eve dinner. That's why she loves designing tableware. "Creating a special setting for the holiday table contributes to the sensory experience of the entire season," she says.

A TASTE OF CHRISTMAS

Ham and Cheese Potato Bites

Mini Turkey Sandwiches

Cranberry Tapenade

Sourdough-Sausage Quiches

CAPTURE THE ESSENCE OF CHRISTMAS with these mouth-watering morsels. This hors d'oeuvre party menu puts a twist on traditional Christmas dinner ingredients. Here they appear in serving sizes just right for a tasting buffet.

Menu
Serves 12 to 16

Cranberry Tapenade
Sourdough-Sausage Quiches
Mini Turkey Sandwiches
Ham and Cheese Potato Bites
Pumpkin Pie Biscotti
Maple-Pecan Tartlets
Iced Eggnog   Hot Coffee

Cranberry Tapenade

Cranberry Tapenade
Purchased sweet potato chips make sturdy dippers for this festive red relish.

1 small sweet potato (about 6 ounces)
1 small navel orange, unpeeled and quartered
2 cups fresh or frozen cranberries
½ cup sugar
2 jalapeño peppers, halved lengthwise and seeded
½ cup chopped pecans, toasted
3 tablespoons chopped fresh cilantro
⅛ teaspoon salt
⅛ teaspoon ground cinnamon
  Sweet potato chips (see Sources on page 154)
  Garnishes: additional cranberries, fresh cilantro sprigs

Cook sweet potato in a small amount of boiling water just until barely tender. Drain and cool completely. Peel and finely dice sweet potato; set aside.

Position knife blade in food processor bowl; add orange quarters. Process until coarsely chopped, stopping once to scrape down sides. Add 2 cups cranberries, sugar, and jalapeño pepper; pulse 2 or 3 times until mixture is finely chopped.

Transfer mixture to a bowl; stir in reserved sweet potato, pecans, and next 3 ingredients. Cover and chill at least 1 hour. Serve with sweet potato chips. Garnish, if desired. **Yield:** 2¼ cups.

Sourdough-Sausage Quiches

These toasty little pastries laced with sage and sausage conjure the taste of turkey dressing.

2 (16-ounce) loaves sliced sourdough bread
⅓ cup butter or margarine, melted
   Vegetable cooking spray
¼ pound hot ground pork sausage
¼ cup minced celery
3 tablespoons minced onion
3 large eggs, lightly beaten
¾ cup half-and-half
½ cup (2 ounces) finely shredded mozzarella
   cheese
½ teaspoon poultry seasoning
¼ teaspoon salt
¼ teaspoon pepper
⅛ teaspoon rubbed sage
   Garnish: celery leaves

Cut bread slices into 40 rounds, using a 3" biscuit cutter. Roll each bread round lightly with a rolling pin. Brush both sides of each round lightly with melted butter. Press into miniature (1¾") muffin pans lightly coated with cooking spray. Bake at 350° for 20 minutes or until crisp and golden.

Cook sausage, celery, and onion in a skillet over medium-high heat until sausage is browned, stirring until sausage is finely crumbled; drain.

Combine sausage mixture, eggs, and next 6 ingredients in a medium bowl; stir well. Spoon into prepared toast cups, filling three-fourths full.

Bake at 350° for 15 minutes or until set. Serve warm. Garnish, if desired. **Yield:** 40 appetizers.

Mini Turkey Sandwiches

1 (7- or 8-ounce) package small party rolls on
   aluminum tray
½ (3-ounce) package cream cheese, softened
2 tablespoons mayonnaise
2 tablespoons sour cream
1 tablespoon chutney
¼ teaspoon curry powder
¼ teaspoon ground red pepper
¼ pound very thinly sliced smoked turkey
½ cup whole berry cranberry sauce
2 tablespoons minced onion

Remove rolls from aluminum tray. Slice rolls in half horizontally, using a serrated knife. Return bottom halves of rolls to tray.

Combine cream cheese, mayonnaise, and sour cream. Beat at low speed of an electric mixer until smooth. Stir in chutney, curry powder, and red pepper. Spread chutney mixture on cut sides of top halves of rolls. Set aside.

Place turkey on bottom halves of rolls. Combine cranberry sauce and onion; stir well. Spread cranberry mixture over turkey. Cover with tops of rolls. (You'll cut sandwiches apart after baking.)

Cover and bake at 350° for 20 to 30 minutes or until sandwiches are thoroughly heated. To serve, cut sandwiches apart with a sharp knife. **Yield:** 2 dozen.

Ham and Cheese Potato Bites

Traditionally, pineapple rings decorate a whole ham. Here, chopped ham and crushed pineapple mingle with a cheese filling in tiny stuffed roasted potatoes.

1½ pounds small unpeeled new potatoes
1 cup (4 ounces) shredded Gruyère cheese
½ cup finely chopped cooked ham
¼ cup plus 2 tablespoons sour cream
¼ cup plus 2 tablespoons soft cream cheese with
   chives and onions
3 tablespoons crushed pineapple, drained well
½ teaspoon garlic salt
½ teaspoon ground red pepper
   Garnish: fresh parsley sprigs

Place potatoes in a lightly greased roasting pan. Bake at 400° for 50 minutes or just until tender. Let cool. Cut potatoes in half. Using a small spoon, scoop out most of pulp from each potato half. Set shells aside.

Combine potato pulp, Gruyère cheese, and next 6 ingredients; stir mixture well. Spoon mixture into potato shells. (You can make the potato bites ahead up to this point and store them in the refrigerator overnight.)

Place potatoes on a rack in a roasting pan. Broil 5½" from heat (with electric oven door partially opened) 4 to 5 minutes or until golden. Garnish, if desired. **Yield:** about 2 dozen.

Pumpkin Pie Biscotti

Maple-Pecan Tartlets

Pumpkin Pie Biscotti

This twice-baked cookie with staying power makes enough extras to package and send as gifts.

3½ cups all-purpose flour
1½ cups firmly packed brown sugar
 2 teaspoons baking powder
½ teaspoon salt
 2 teaspoons pumpkin pie spice
½ cup canned, mashed pumpkin
 2 large eggs, lightly beaten
 1 tablespoon vanilla extract
 2 tablespoons butter or margarine
1¼ cups macadamia nuts, coarsely chopped

Combine first 5 ingredients in a large bowl; stir well. Combine pumpkin, eggs, and vanilla, stirring well with a wire whisk. Slowly add pumpkin mixture to flour mixture, stirring until dry ingredients are moistened. (Mixture will be very crumbly; it will gradually become moist after stirring.)

 Melt butter in a large skillet over medium heat; add macadamia nuts. Cook, stirring constantly, until nuts are browned. Remove from heat, and cool completely. Knead or gently stir cooled nuts into dough.

 Place dough on a lightly floured surface, and divide into 4 portions. Lightly flour hands, and shape each portion into a 1" x 15" log. Place logs 3" apart on lightly greased large cookie sheets.

 Bake at 350° for 23 minutes; cool logs 15 minutes. Reduce oven temperature to 300°.

 Cut each log crosswise into ½" slices, using a serrated knife. Place slices on ungreased cookie sheets. Bake at 300° for 15 minutes. Cool completely on wire racks. **Yield:** 8 dozen.

Maple-Pecan Tartlets

Ground cinnamon in the cream cheese pastry makes these petite pies something to write home about.

¾ cup firmly packed brown sugar
¼ cup maple syrup
 1 tablespoon butter or margarine, melted
⅛ teaspoon salt
 1 large egg, lightly beaten
¾ cup finely chopped pecans, toasted
   Cinnamon Pastry Shells

Combine first 5 ingredients in a small mixing bowl; beat at medium speed of an electric mixer until blended. Stir in pecans. Spoon filling evenly into Cinnamon Pastry Shells.

Bake at 325° for 25 minutes or until set. Cool slightly. Remove from pans, and cool completely on a wire rack. **Yield:** 2 dozen.

Cinnamon Pastry Shells
1 (3-ounce) package cream cheese, softened
⅓ cup butter or margarine, softened
1 cup all-purpose flour
¾ teaspoon ground cinnamon

Beat cream cheese and butter at medium speed of an electric mixer until creamy. Gradually add flour and cinnamon, beating at low speed just until ingredients are blended. Wrap dough in wax paper, and chill 2 hours.

Divide dough in half. Divide each half of dough into 12 balls. Place in lightly greased miniature (1¾") muffin pans, shaping each into a shell. **Yield:** 2 dozen.

Iced Eggnog
Here's a rich takeoff on iced coffee. Vanilla-rum ice cream cubes melt quickly to provide a punch of flavor.

3½ cups vanilla ice cream, softened
½ cup dark rum
2 quarts refrigerated eggnog
Freshly ground nutmeg

Combine softened ice cream and rum; stir until blended. Spoon mixture into ice cube trays. (You should be able to make about 28 ice cream cubes.) Freeze at least 8 hours. (Ice cream cubes will not freeze hard like ice. You'll be able to remove them as soft cubes.)

Fill individual glasses two-thirds full with eggnog. Add 2 or 3 ice cream cubes to each glass. Sprinkle with nutmeg. Serve immediately. **Yield**: 8 cups.

Note: You can combine the eggnog and ice cream cubes in a punch bowl and serve with a ladle, if desired.

Iced Eggnog

COFFEE CHARMS

Menu
Serves 12 to 16
Brown Sugar-Cinnamon Pecans
Mocha Fondue
Slice 'n' Bake Coffee Cookies
Coffee Bars
German Chocolate Truffles
Rum-Glazed Coffee Rolls
Frosted Coffee   Hot Coffee

German
Chocolate
Truffles

Brown Sugar-
Cinnamon Pecans

Coffee Bars

Slice 'n' Bake Coffee
Cookies

Frosted Coffee

FOR AN EVENING BRIMMING WITH holiday appeal, brew up a coffee-and-sweets soiree. This menu spotlights coffee—from chocolate-covered beans to Kahlúa to ice cream. You can make several recipes ahead. Double them to yield enough for party favors.

Brown Sugar-Cinnamon Pecans

 2 tablespoons butter or margarine
¼ cup firmly packed brown sugar
 1 tablespoon pecan-praline-flavored ground coffee
 2 tablespoons orange juice
½ teaspoon ground cinnamon
¼ teaspoon ground red pepper
 2 cups pecan halves

Rum-Glazed
Coffee Rolls

German
Chocolate Truffles

Melt butter in a large skillet over medium heat; add brown sugar and next 4 ingredients. Stir well. Add pecans, stirring well to coat. Remove from heat.

Spread coated pecans on a lightly greased 15" x 10" x 1" jellyroll pan. Bake at 325° for 14 to 15 minutes, stirring every 5 minutes. Cool completely. Break nuts apart. **Yield:** 2 cups.

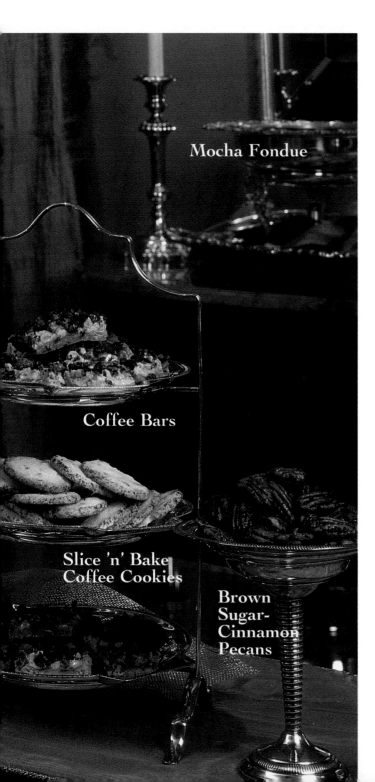

Mocha Fondue

Coffee Bars

Slice 'n' Bake Coffee Cookies

Brown Sugar-Cinnamon Pecans

Mocha Fondue

1 (14-ounce) can sweetened condensed milk
1 (12-ounce) package semisweet chocolate morsels
1 cup miniature marshmallows
¼ cup strong brewed coffee
⅓ cup Kahlúa or other coffee-flavored liqueur
   Pound cake cubes
   Angel food cake cubes
   Apple and pear slices

Combine first 4 ingredients in a medium saucepan; cook, stirring constantly, over medium-low heat until chocolate melts and mixture is smooth. Stir in Kahlúa. Pour mixture into fondue pot; place over fondue burner. Serve with cake cubes and fruit as dippers. **Yield:** 3 cups.

Slice 'n' Bake Coffee Cookies

½ cup unsalted butter, softened
1 cup sugar
1 large egg
1 teaspoon vanilla extract
2 cups all-purpose flour
1 teaspoon baking powder
¼ teaspoon salt
¾ cup toasted and skinned whole hazelnuts, chopped
¼ cup sugar
1 tablespoon hazelnut-flavored instant coffee granules

Beat butter at medium speed of an electric mixer until creamy; gradually add 1 cup sugar, beating well. Add egg and vanilla, beating until blended.

Combine flour, baking powder, and salt; add to butter mixture, beating well. Stir in hazelnuts. Divide dough in half; shape into 11" logs.

Combine ¼ cup sugar and coffee granules; stir well. Roll each log in sugar mixture, coating heavily. Wrap each log in wax paper. Chill logs until firm.

Cut dough into ¼" thick slices, and place on ungreased cookie sheets. Bake at 350° for 8 to 10 minutes or until lightly browned. Remove to wire racks, and cool completely. Store in an airtight container up to 1 week. **Yield:** 6 dozen.

Coffee Bars

The rocky tops on these luscious bar cookies come from chocolate-covered coffee beans and crushed toffee bars.

¾ cup butter or margarine, softened
¾ cup firmly packed brown sugar
1 egg yolk
1½ cups all-purpose flour
1 tablespoon instant coffee granules
¼ teaspoon salt
1 (14-ounce) can sweetened condensed milk
2 tablespoons butter or margarine
1 tablespoon Kahlúa or strong brewed coffee
1 cup chopped walnuts
1 cup chocolate-covered coffee beans, chopped
1 cup coarsely chopped English toffee-flavored candy bars

Beat ¾ cup butter at medium speed of an electric mixer until creamy; gradually add brown sugar, beating well. Add egg yolk, beating well. Add flour, coffee granules, and salt, stirring just until blended. Using greased fingers, press dough into bottom of a lightly greased 13" x 9" x 2" pan. Bake at 350° for 20 minutes. Set aside.

Combine sweetened condensed milk and 2 tablespoons butter in a saucepan. Bring to a boil over medium heat; cook 5 minutes, stirring often. Remove from heat, and stir in Kahlúa. Pour mixture over prepared crust. Sprinkle with walnuts.

Bake at 350° for 10 to 12 minutes or until golden. Remove from oven. Sprinkle with chopped coffee beans and toffee bars while still warm. Cool completely in pan on a wire rack. Cover and chill until firm. Let stand 5 minutes before cutting into bars. **Yield:** 3 dozen.

German Chocolate Truffles

For an effortless centerpiece, pile truffles in wine goblets that have shimmery holiday ribbons tied to their stems.

1 cup sifted powdered sugar, divided
1½ tablespoons German chocolate-flavored coffee granules (see Sources on page 154)
1 (4-ounce) bar sweet baking chocolate, chopped
1 (3-ounce) package cream cheese, softened
½ teaspoon coconut extract
Coatings: chocolate sprinkles, flaked coconut

Position knife blade in a miniature food processor bowl; add ¼ cup powdered sugar and coffee granules. Process until mixture resembles a fine powder; set aside.

Melt chocolate in a heavy saucepan over low heat, stirring often. Remove from heat, and cool slightly.

Combine reserved powdered sugar mixture, melted chocolate, remaining ¾ cup powdered sugar, cream cheese, and coconut extract in a medium bowl; beat at medium speed of an electric mixer until smooth. Cover and chill 30 minutes.

Shape mixture into 1" balls; roll in desired coatings. **Yield:** about 2 dozen.

Truffle-coating variation:
Combine 1 (12-ounce) package semisweet chocolate morsels and 1½ tablespoons shortening in top of a double boiler over hot, not simmering, water. Cook until chocolate melts. Dip uncoated truffles into chocolate mixture, coating completely. Place on wax paper to dry.

Place 2 ounces white chocolate baking squares in top of double boiler over hot, not simmering, water. Cook until white chocolate melts. Cool slightly. Spoon into a small zip-top plastic bag, and seal. Snip a tiny hole in 1 corner of bag. Drizzle white chocolate over chocolate-coated truffles.

Rum-Glazed Coffee Rolls

Don't worry about how you arrange these sugar-coated biscuits in the pan—during baking they expand into a coffee cake that separates easily into single rolls.

½ cup coarsely chopped pecans
1 cup firmly packed brown sugar
⅓ cup brewed coffee
¼ cup butter or margarine, melted
2 tablespoons dark rum
⅔ cup sugar
2 tablespoons instant coffee granules
2 (11-ounce) cans refrigerated buttermilk biscuits
⅓ cup butter or margarine, melted

Sprinkle pecans in a heavily greased 12-cup Bundt pan. Combine brown sugar and next 3 ingredients, stirring well. Pour mixture into pan.

Combine ⅔ cup sugar and coffee granules in a shallow bowl; stir well. Separate biscuits; dip biscuits in ⅓ cup melted butter, and dredge in sugar mixture. Stand biscuits on edge around pan, placing 12 on outer side and 8 on inner side of pan.

Bake at 350° for 28 minutes. Cool in pan on a wire rack 5 minutes. Invert onto a serving platter, and serve immediately. **Yield:** 20 rolls.

Frosted Coffee

You can double this thick, icy concoction to serve a crowd; just be sure to prepare it in batches. Spoon immediately into frosty pitchers for serving—it melts quickly.

3 cups coffee ice cream
¼ cup hot fudge topping
¼ teaspoon ground cinnamon
3 cups small ice cubes
Garnish: maraschino cherries with stems

Combine first 3 ingredients in container of an electric blender; cover and process just until blended, stopping once to scrape down sides. Turn blender on high; gradually add ice, blending until smooth. Garnish, if desired. Serve immediately. **Yield:** 4 cups.

Rum-Glazed
Coffee Rolls

Spiced Fruit

DECORATIONS

Hang the stocking with care and place the wreath on the door. In the following pages, we have ideas for these plus instructions for a stenciled Christmas cushion, bottle toppers, and the fragrant fruit you see here.

Spiced Fruit

PLASTIC APPLES AND PEARS CLOAKED IN fragrant cinnamon, ginger, and allspice are a twist on traditional potpourri. Set in a dish or a bowl, the spicy still life will scent your home all holiday long.

You will need (for 3 apples, 1 pear, and 1 pear cluster):
3 (3" x 3½") plastic apples
1 (3¼" x 4") plastic pear
1 small cluster of plastic pears
metal skewers
acrylic paints in colors to match cinnamon, ginger, and allspice
thick craft glue
½"-wide artist's paintbrush
1 (1-ounce) container each powdered cinnamon, ginger, and allspice
hot-glue gun with glue sticks
small twigs
whole bay leaves

1. To prepare fruit, remove top and bottom stems; discard. Wash and dry fruit. Insert skewers into stem holes for temporary handles.

2. To coat fruit, mix 1 part paint with 2 parts craft glue. Use cinnamon-colored paint for apples, ginger-colored paint for pear, and allspice-colored paint for pear cluster. For each fruit, paint surface with mixture, covering evenly and completely. Touch up any missed spots. Sprinkle thick, even coating of spice onto wet paint, completely covering surface. Use cinnamon for apples, ginger for pear, and allspice for pear cluster. Using fingertips, gently pat spice to adhere firmly. Let dry several hours. Gently tap skewer to dislodge excess spice. Carefully remove skewer.

3. To add stems and leaves, hot-glue small twig to each fruit for stem. Hot-glue bay leaves to each stem as desired.

Velvet and Organza Stocking

This stunning stocking is the height of elegance, but its upturned toe adds an amusing kick.

You will need:
pattern and diagram on page 152
graph paper with 1" grid
½ yard velvet for stocking
¾ yard organza for cuff
9" length gold braid for hanger
¼ yard lining fabric to match stocking

Note: All seam allowances are ⅝". For velvet, see Sources on page 154.

1. To make stocking, using graph paper and pattern on page 152, enlarge stocking pattern. Transfer all pattern markings. From velvet, cut 1 stocking piece. Reverse pattern and cut 1 more. With right sides facing and raw edges aligned, stitch stocking pieces together, leaving top edge open. Clip curves. Turn right side out. Press.

2. To make cuff, from organza, cut 2 (9" x 42") cuff pieces and 1 (7" x 14") piece for cuff stay. With right sides facing and raw edges aligned, stitch 9" x 42" organza pieces together along short ends to make a tube. For cuff stay, with right sides facing and raw edges aligned, fold 7" x 14" in half widthwise. Stitch short ends together.

Along top and bottom edges of cuff, stitch 2 rows of gathering stitches, ½" and ⅜" from each edge. Pull threads to gather 1 edge of cuff, adjusting gathers evenly. With right sides facing, raw edges aligned, and seams matching, stitch gathered edge of cuff to 1 edge of cuff stay. Trim seam. Understitch seam allowance to cuff stay.

3. To attach cuff to stocking, with right sides facing, raw edges aligned, and cuff stay seam matching 1 stocking side seam, pin remaining edge of stay to top edge of stocking. Baste in place (see diagram). Gather remaining edge of cuff, adjusting gathers evenly. Pin cuff to top of stocking, on top of stay, matching seams to stocking side seams. Baste in place.

4. To make hanger, fold gold braid in half, aligning ends. With raw edges aligned, baste loop to right side of stocking at side seam.

5. To cut and attach lining, using stocking pattern, from lining, cut 2 stocking pieces from top to cutting line indicated on pattern. (Lining does not extend into foot of stocking.) Be sure to notch stocking lining where indicated.

With right sides facing and raw edges aligned, stitch lining pieces together at sides, leaving top and bottom edges open. If desired, clean-finish bottom (unnotched) edge of lining. (Clean-finish by serging or stitching a narrow hem or by pinking.) With right sides facing, raw top edges aligned, and sides seams and notch matching, slip lining over stocking and cuff. Stitch. Turn lining to inside. On inside, tack lining side seams to stocking side seam allowances.

Duffy Morrison of Shelby, Alabama, says she loves making gifts because "handwork personalizes the gift to the receiver." Look for more of her whimsical stocking designs on page 98.

Christmas Card Screen

Tuck your holiday cards under the ribbons on this Gothic-arched screen. After the holidays, use it as a memo board or a decoration for a sideboard or an empty corner.

You will need:
pattern on page 152
graph paper with 1" grid
3 (36") lengths 1 x 12 shelving
jigsaw or band saw
sandpaper
2½ yards 54"-wide fabric (Yardage may vary depending on pattern repeats.)
medium-weight polyester batting
staple gun and ¼" staples
4 (2") brass middle hinges
10 yards ½"-wide grosgrain ribbon
hot-glue gun and glue sticks
7½ yards gimp
fabric glue
felt (optional)

Note: For fabric, see Sources on page 154.

1. To cut panels, using pattern on page 152 and saw, shape top and bottom of each length of shelving. Sand rough edges.

2. To cover panels, cut 6 (3 front and 3 back) approximately 15" x 40" lengths from fabric, taking care to align patterns across front and back if necessary. Cut 6 panels of batting to same measurements. Trim ¼" from edges to prevent seams from becoming bulky.

Layer batting and fabric right side up on top of 1 panel. Pull fabric taut and wrap to edges of panel. Staple in place along side edges of panel first and then along top. Do not staple bottom at this time. Trim excess fabric ⅛" from stapled edges. Repeat to cover remaining side of panel.

At bottom of panel, trim batting pieces even with bottom edge. Turn under each raw edge of fabric. Staple each to bottom edge of panel, pulling fabric taut as you staple. Trim excess fabric ⅛" from stapled edges. Repeat to cover remaining 2 panels.

3. To attach hinges, place panels right side up. Measure and mark 3" and 26" from bottom edge along both sides of middle panel. Repeat to mark right edge of first panel and left edge of last panel. Align bottom end of hinges with these marks and screw to panels.

4. To create ribbon grid, starting at bottom of first panel, cut ribbons and place approximately 8½" apart in trellis pattern, leaving approximately 2" extending off panel at each side. Hot-glue ribbons in place at edges of panel. Trim ribbon ends. Repeat to form ribbon grid across middle and last panel.

5. To finish, using fabric glue, attach gimp around edges of panels to conceal staples and ribbon ends. Glue felt to bottom of panels to prevent scratches if desired.

Harlequin Tray

Treat your guests with this fanciful server, which is actually an ordinary baking sheet transformed with paint.

You will need:
13" x 9" x 2" baking sheet
enamel paints: antique gold, flat black
paintbrushes
clear polyurethane spray (optional)

1. **To mark diamonds,** using pencil, lightly draw line across width of baking sheet to mark center. Measure and mark 2" intervals on each side of center line to ends of tray, leaving ½" margin at each end. To form diamonds, lightly draw diagonal lines across baking sheet from top of each 2" mark to bottom of adjacent mark on each side of each mark. For each end of baking sheet, extend diamond design up side and onto handle (see photo).

2. **To paint diamonds,** using paintbrush or fingertips and antique gold paint, paint inside marked diamonds. Apply 2 to 3 coats, letting dry between each coat.

3. **To paint swirl designs,** using black paint and paintbrush, paint swirl freehand in center of each diamond. Let dry. If desired, spray with clear polyurethane to protect finish. Let dry.

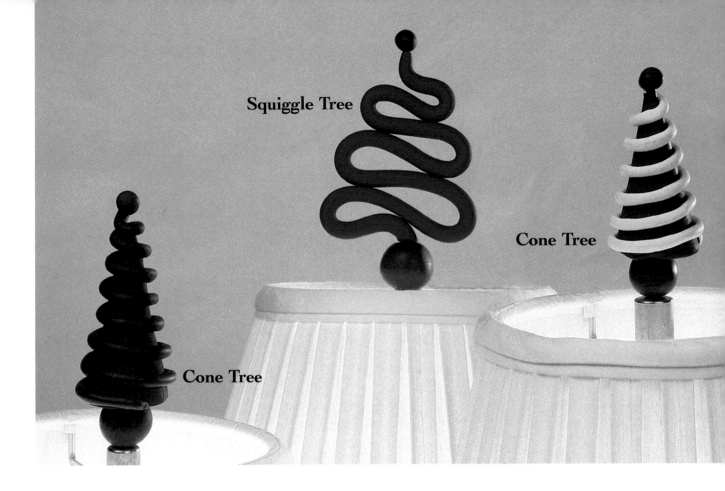

Squiggle Tree

Cone Tree

Cone Tree

Festive Finials & Bottle Toppers

Make a holiday statement with craft clay. It's as easy—and as fun—as rolling out cookie dough.

You will need:
rubber gloves
craft clay: green, red, white (Sculpey III used)
craft knife
heavy-duty glue
flat-topped plain lamp finial (for each finial)
cork (for each bottle topper)
liquid leaf paints: gold, silver
paintbrush

Note: For all clay projects, bake at 275° for about 20 minutes and let cool for 20 minutes. Wear rubber gloves while handling clay to prevent leaving finger-prints. For craft clay, see Sources on page 154.

Squiggle Tree

1. **To make tree,** roll green clay into ball. Form ball into ¼"-wide and 14"-long log. Slightly taper 1 end for tree top. Referring to photo and starting at top, shape log into squiggle on baking sheet. Using craft knife, trim excess clay.

2. **To make tree topper and base,** roll red clay into 1 (1"-diameter) ball and 1 (¼"-diameter) ball. For flat gluing surfaces, tap top and bottom of large ball on flat surface.

3. **To finish,** bake all clay pieces. Let cool. Glue small ball to tree top and large ball to tree bottom. Let dry. Glue onto lamp finial. Let dry.

Cone Tree

1. To make tree, roll green clay into large ball. Form ball into 3"-high cone, evening sides on flat surface. Bake upright on sheet in oven. Let cool.

2. To make tree topper and base, roll clay into 1 (¼"-diameter) ball and 1 (½"-diameter) ball. For flat gluing surfaces, tap 1 side of small ball and top and bottom of large ball on flat surface.

3. To make squiggle, roll clay into large ball. Form ball into ⅛"-wide and 15"-long log. Slightly taper 1 end for tree top. When cone is cool, attach tapered end of log to top of cone. Turning cone in hand, wind log down cone, making sure log is evenly spaced (see photo). Using craft knife, trim excess log, cutting at angle. Press end into cone.

4. To finish, bake all clay pieces, including baked cone. Let cool. Glue small ball to cone top and large ball to cone bottom. Let dry. Glue onto lamp finial. Let dry.

Star Squiggle, Ball Twist, and Curl

1. To make squiggle, roll white clay into ¾"-diameter ball. Form ball into ½"-wide and 5"-long log, tapering 1 end. For flat gluing surfaces, tap log ends on flat surface. Shape log into squiggle on baking sheet (see photo).
To make star, roll white clay into 1"-diameter ball. Using fingertips, evenly press ball flat onto baking sheet. Using craft knife, cut out star. Loosen star from baking sheet.

2. To make ball twist, roll white clay into 2 (1"-diameter) balls. Form 1 ball into ¼"-wide and 8"-long log. Wrap middle of log around remaining ball, twisting ends of log together beneath ball. Using craft knife, cut twist to desired length.

3. To make curl, roll white clay into 1"-diameter ball. Form ball into ½"-wide and 5"-long log, tapering 1 end. For flat gluing surface, tap other log end on flat surface. Shape log into curl on baking sheet (see photo).

Ball Twist

Curl

Star Squiggle

4. To make each base, roll white clay into ¾"-diameter balls. For squiggle base, roll 2 balls, pressing 1 ball into disk shape. Form other ball into ¼"-wide and 1"-long log. Wrap log around base of squiggle to form collar. Remove collar (retaining shape) before baking and lay flat on sheet to bake separately. To make ball twist base, press 2 balls into disk shape; sandwich 1 ball between disks. To make curl base, press 2 balls into disk shapes, making 1 disk thicker.

5. To finish, bake all clay items. Let cool. Glue each design to base. Glue base together and then glue onto cork. Let dry.

6. To paint, use gold liquid leaf to paint curl and star squiggle. Use silver liquid leaf to paint ball twist. Let dry.

Golden Angel Pillow and Ornament

Use our celestial stencil to adorn a pair of heavenly accessories.

Pillow

You will need (for both projects):
pattern on page 145
8½" x 11" sheet plastic template material
protective mat or cardboard
craft knife
waxed paper (to protect work surface)
¾ yard 45"-wide fabric (ivory raw silk used)
gold acrylic fabric paint
silver glitter paint
stencil brush
polyester stuffing
gold trim (for pillow)
hot-glue gun and glue sticks (for pillow)
white and gold pearls by the yard (for ornament)

Stenciling Instructions

1. To make stencil, using pattern, trace angel onto frosted side of plastic. Place plastic, shiny side up, on protective mat. Cut out stencil, using craft knife.

2. To prepare surface for stenciling, tape large pieces of waxed paper to work surface. If desired, practice stenciling on muslin scraps.

3. To stencil, place material to be stenciled on top of waxed paper. Place stencil in desired position. Using stencil brush and paint, stencil pattern onto material. Let dry.

Pillow

Note: Finished pillow is 10" x 14". All seam allowances are ¼".

1. To cut out pillow, cut 2 (10½" x 14½") rectangles from fabric.

2. To stencil, using gold paint for angel and silver paint for stars, stencil 2 designs on right side of 1 rectangle. Reverse stencil for 1 design so that angels face each other (see photo). Let dry.

3. To make pillow, with right sides facing and raw edges aligned, stitch rectangles together, leaving large opening. Clip corners and turn. Stuff to desired fullness. Slipstitch opening closed. Hot-glue trim to pillow edges. Let dry.

Ornament

Ornament

1. To stencil ornament, cut 2 (7") squares from fabric. Using gold paint for angel and silver paint for stars, stencil design on right side of 1 square. Let dry. With wrong sides together and raw edges aligned, place painted square faceup on top of remaining square. Trim around stenciled shape, leaving ¼" for seam allowance.

2. To make ornament, with right sides facing and raw edges aligned, stitch pieces together, leaving small opening. Clip corners and turn. Stuff to desired fullness. Slipstitch opening closed.

3. To add pearl trim, beginning and ending at side of angel head, tack white pearl strand around edges of ornament, leaving 8" free at end for hanger (see photo). Tack free end to ornament to make loop. Referring to photo, tack gold pearl strand in swirling design for hair. If desired, tack individual pearls to stars.

Patina-look Holly Garland

Paper Bag Holly Garlands

THESE GARLANDS, FASHIONED FROM brown paper bags and glue, feature pliable stems for flexible decorating options.

You will need (for 2 garlands):
patterns and diagrams on page 144
2 heavy-duty brown paper grocery bags
18-gauge florist's wire: 64 (6") lengths for leaves,
    2 (36") lengths for garland
Aleene's Tacky Glue™
candle
muslin scrap
70 (4") lengths 22-gauge florist's wire
70 (6-mm) wooden beads
acrylic paints: black, burgundy, red, metallic
    copper, dark green, medium green, bright
    green, metallic gold, blue-green, white
paintbrush
pop-up craft sponge
green florist's tape

Note: Make garland longer or shorter than 36" by adjusting length of 18-gauge florist's wire. Don't forget to adjust number of leaves and berry clusters.

    1. To make each leaf, cut 2 (3½" x 4½") pieces of brown bag. Using patterns, transfer 1 pattern to 1 brown bag piece, aligning straight bottom edge of pattern with 1 (3½") edge. With edges aligned and pattern faceup, stack bag pieces and sandwich 1 (6") length of 18-gauge wire in between. Leaving 3½" extending beyond paper edge, align wire with dotted center line. Glue stacked bag pieces together, encasing wire. Let dry about 5 minutes. Cut out.

Green Holly Garland

Repeat to make total of 6 small leaves and 26 large leaves. Shape leaves as desired. Let dry.

2. To burn each leaf, spread fairly thick coat of glue on 1 side of leaf. While glue is still wet, hold leaf, glue side down, over candle flame. Hold leaf as close as possible to flame without snuffing out flame. Move leaf around over flame until all glue is black and sooty. (Burning process takes 1½ to 2 minutes and will produce some smoke.)

Using muslin scrap, gently wipe off soot. If any brown bag shows through, glue is not completely burned; hold leaf over flame again to complete burning process. To create textured surface, use muslin scrap to mold soft glue, slightly ruffling surface. Let dry overnight.

3. To make each berry, bend 1 (4") length of 22-gauge wire in half. Push folded end of wire through hole in 1 bead (see diagrams). Squeeze bit of glue into hole in bead. Let dry.

4. To paint leaves and berries, paint beads and back of each leaf black. Let dry. For red holly berries, sponge-paint each berry with burgundy and red. Let dry. For copper holly berries, sponge-paint each berry with metallic copper. Let dry.

For green holly leaves, lightly sponge-paint front and back of each leaf with dark green, medium green, and bright green (see photo), letting 1 side dry before painting the other. Lightly sponge-paint edge of each leaf with metallic gold. Let dry. **For patina-look holly leaves,** lightly sponge-paint front and back of each leaf with metallic copper, blue-green, and white, letting 1 side dry before painting the other. Let dry.

5. To assemble garland, using florist's tape, wrap 1" to 2" of free end of each stem (see diagram). Attach leaves and berries to 36" length of 18-gauge wire with tape, arranging smaller leaves at ends of garland and using 2 or 3 berries for clusters between leaves. (Remember that florist's tape must be stretched as it is wrapped to make it stick to itself.)

Decorate with Decoupage

CUT LOOSE WITH ILLUSTRATIONS FROM old Christmas cards or calendars to make this holiday mantel trio.

Reverse Decoupage Plate

You will need:
clear glass plate
wrapping paper for border
cutout paper designs for center
white glue
sponge paintbrush
gold tissue for plate base
felt for plate base

1. **To apply cutout designs,** wash and dry glass plate. Trim wrapping paper to fit plate border. Arrange cutouts on plate to determine placement. Use sponge brush to apply glue evenly to printed side of each border piece and cutout. Position border pieces and cutouts on back of glass plate so that printed design is visible from front of plate. Gently flatten border pieces and cutouts, smoothing any air bubbles. Use damp paper towel to remove excess glue. Let dry.

2. **To apply tissue and felt,** make paper pattern equal to base of plate (not including border). Trace pattern 1 time each onto tissue and felt. Cut out. Brush glue onto underside base of plate. Press tissue onto glue-covered area, aligning edges. Gently flatten tissue, smoothing any air bubbles. Let dry. (*Note:* Some wrinkling may occur with tissue, but this will only add interesting texture to design.) Brush glue onto back of tissue. Press felt onto glue-covered area, aligning edges. Let dry.

Decoupaged Candlesticks

Decoupaged Candlesticks

You will need:
candlesticks suitable for decoupaging
decoupage glue (Aleene's Instant Decoupage Glue and Finish™ used)
sponge paintbrush
cutout paper designs from gift wrap, greeting cards, and decorative papers

Reverse Decoupage Plate

1. To prepare surface of each candlestick, using sponge brush, apply 1 coat of decoupage glue to entire surface. Let dry.

2. To apply cutout designs to each candlestick, arrange cutouts to determine placement. For each cutout, use sponge brush to apply coat of decoupage glue at desired position. Press cutout onto glue-covered area. Gently flatten cutout, smoothing any air bubbles. Brush coat of decoupage glue on top of cutout, covering edges. Apply additional cutouts, 1 at a time, in same manner until desired effect is achieved. Let dry.

Snowflake Pillow Wrap

Star Pillow Wrap

Christmassy Pillow Wraps

Tie on a holiday look with these quick-and-easy cover-ups. We used wool, but you can try felt or luxurious Ultrasuede. Your best bet is a fabric that does not ravel easily.

You will need:
patterns and diagrams on pages 150 and 151
⅓ yard red wool (for star wrap)
⅓ yard blue wool (for snowflake wrap)
fusible web
tracing paper
craft knife
white marking pencil

Star Pillow Wrap

1. To cut fabric, from red wool, cut 4 (10") squares and 6 (2" x 8") rectangles. From fusible web, cut 2 (10") squares.

Following manufacturer's instructions, with wrong sides together and raw edges aligned, fuse pairs of red squares together. Using matching thread, blanket-stitch along edge of each square. Stitch rectangles in same manner.

2. To make star, using pattern on page 150, trace star. Cut out, using craft knife. Center star on 1 square and, using white pencil, transfer design onto wool. Using matching thread, blanket-stitch just inside marked outline. Cut out center with craft knife (see photo).

3. To assemble pillow wrap, slightly overlap squares at bottom point of star square. Sew squares together as shown in Diagram 1, using straight stitch.

4. To attach ties, pleat 1 end of 1 rectangle into thirds. Position tie ½" under 1 point of square. Stitch in place as shown in Diagram 2, using straight stitch. Repeat with remaining rectangles and remaining points. Tie finished pillow wrap around 12"-square pillow (see photo).

Snowflake Pillow Wrap

1. To cut fabric, from blue wool, cut 8 (2" x 8") rectangles and 2 (11" x 29") rectangles. From fusible web, cut 1 (11" x 29") rectangle.

Following manufacturer's instructions, with wrong sides together and raw edges aligned, fuse 11" x 29" rectangles together.

2. To make snowflake, using pattern on page 151, trace snowflake. Cut out, using craft knife. Position jagged edge of snowflake pattern at 1 end of fused rectangle, with tips of jagged points touching edge of fabric. Tape pattern in place. Using white pencil, transfer design onto wool. Using matching thread, blanket-stitch along straight and jagged edges of rectangle. Cut out snowflake pattern, using craft knife (see photo).

3. To attach ties, pleat 1 end of 1 (2" x 8") rectangle into thirds. Position tie ½" under rectangle at 1 side of jagged end (see Diagram 3). Stitch to rectangle as shown in Diagram 2, using straight stitch. Repeat with remaining 2" x 8" rectangles (see Diagram 3). Tie finished pillow wrap around 12"-square pillow (see photo).

Linda Hendrickson of Arlington, Virginia, chose simple cookie cutter shapes and cozy wool fabrics for her pillow designs to "visually ward off the chill of a cold winter day and quickly add a Christmas look to any room."

Oak Leaf Wreath

Select oak leaves in midsummer to craft this naturally beautiful decoration. Wire the delicate circlet to an evergreen wreath for a grand holiday display.

You will need:
small branches with fresh oak leaves
glycerin (available at drug stores)
gilding compound (Treasure Gold® used):
    #3060 Copper, #3040 White Fire,
    #3030 Renaissance, #3080 Silver
acorns with caps
hot-glue gun and glue sticks
13"-diameter grapevine wreath
20"-diameter evergreen wreath
florist's wire
ribbon

1. To prepare leaves, gather branches in mid-summer when new growth has hardened. Scrape bark from each branch 1" from cut end. Pound area with hammer to loosen fibers and to enable stem to absorb glycerin.

Mix 1 part glycerin with 2 parts water. Pour 1" to 2" of mixture into container. Submerge cut, pounded end of branches in container. Leave branches in glycerin mixture for 6 weeks or until foliage has turned dark brown. Leaves should be supple, not brittle. (Add additional mixture to container if needed during processing.) When leaves are ready, remove from branches. Rinse and dry leaves to remove excess glycerin.

2. To gild leaves, using fingertips, gently rub gilding compound onto fronts and backs of leaves. Use 1 base color and 1 or more accent colors on each leaf, blending colors as desired.

3. To glue leaves to wreath, select 10 leaves of approximate size. (Those shown are about 5½" long.) Hot-glue caps to acorns, if necessary, to secure. Glue bases of acorns together in groups of 3 to make clusters.

Glue leaves in pairs on grapevine wreath. Glue 1 acorn cluster to each pair of leaves, covering area where stem ends cross.

4. To attach oak leaf wreath to evergreen wreath, use florist's wire. Add ribbon bow if desired.

Merry Mailbox Banner

Share your Christmas cheer with passersby with this weatherproof mailbox flag. Use these instructions and two shades of pastel-colored nylon to make a happy birthday banner.

You will need:
1 yard each rip-stop nylon: green, red
1⅔ yards ⅝"-wide green ribbon

Note: All seam allowances are ¼".

1. To cut fabric, from green nylon, cut 2 (20" x 36") pieces. From red nylon, cut 2 (4" x 36") strips, 2 (4" x 20") strips, 2 (14" x 16") strips, and 2 (4" x 8") strips.

2. To assemble banner, center 1 (4" x 36") red strip vertically on right side of 1 green piece. Using narrow zigzag, appliqué red strip to green piece. Center 1 (4" x 20") red strip horizontally across red stitched piece. Zigzag in place. Repeat for remaining green piece.

With right sides together and raw edges aligned, stitch green pieces together along 1 short end. Press. Turn remaining raw edges under ¼" twice and stitch to hem.

3. To make hole for mailbox flag, center banner over mailbox. Mark position of bottom of mailbox flag. Make a buttonhole in banner large enough for flag to pass through.

4. To make bows, with right sides together, fold 1 (14" x 16") red strip in half lengthwise. Stitch, leaving an opening for turning. Turn. Slipstitch opening closed. Press. Fold piece in half widthwise; finger-press to mark center. Run gathering threads along center fold. Pull threads to gather to 3" width at center. Fold 1" of long edges of 1 (4" x 8") red strip to wrong side and press. Wrap around center of gathered piece; slipstitch ends to back of gathered piece. Repeat to make second bow. Slipstitch 1 bow to each side of banner where horizontal and vertical strips meet.

5. To make banner ties, cut ribbon into 4 (15") lengths. Place banner on mailbox with flag through buttonhole. On each long inside edge of banner, mark position for ribbons just below mailbox. Stitch lengths to banner at marks. Tie ribbon ties beneath mailbox to keep banner in place.

Dark Chocolate
Amaretto Cake

SWEETS IN SECONDS

The ingredients are few, and the steps are short. You create these showstoppers with a quick stir of the spatula.

Chocolate Mint Torte

Labor is low, and results are lovely with these dazzling desserts that come easily to your table. Each recipe is a timesaving treasure that tastes totally homemade—but isn't.

Dark Chocolate-Amaretto Cake

You don't need liqueur for this cake. Its subtle amaretto flavor comes from almond extract and flavored coffee creamer.

   1 (18.25-ounce) package devil's food cake mix
     with pudding
   1 (5.9-ounce) package chocolate fudge instant
     pudding mix
1¼ cups water
 ½ cup vegetable oil
   1 tablespoon almond extract
   4 large eggs
   3 cups semisweet chocolate morsels, divided
 ½ cup amaretto-flavored liquid non-dairy
     creamer
   3 tablespoons sliced natural almonds, toasted

Combine first 6 ingredients in a large mixing bowl; beat at medium speed of an electric mixer 2 minutes. Stir in 2 cups chocolate morsels. Pour batter into a greased and floured 12-cup Bundt pan.

Bake at 350° for 55 to 65 minutes or until a wooden pick inserted in center comes out clean. Cool in pan on a wire rack 10 minutes; remove from pan, and cool completely on wire rack.

Combine remaining 1 cup chocolate morsels and amaretto-flavored creamer in a small saucepan. Cook over medium heat, stirring constantly, until chocolate morsels melt. Remove from heat; let stand 15 minutes. Drizzle chocolate glaze over cake; sprinkle with almonds. **Yield:** one 10" cake.

Chocolate Mint Torte

Serve this torte refrigerated or frozen—it's delectable either way.

   1 (15-ounce) loaf fat-free chocolate pound cake
 ¼ cup plus 2 tablespoons chocolate syrup
   1 (4.67-ounce) package chocolate-covered mint
     wafer candies, divided
   1 cup whipping cream
 ¼ cup sifted powdered sugar

Slice pound cake in half horizontally; slice each half in half again horizontally. Brush top of each layer with 1½ tablespoons chocolate syrup; let stand 15 minutes for layers to absorb syrup.

Reserve 8 whole candies for garnish. Finely chop remaining candies.

Combine whipping cream and powdered sugar in a large mixing bowl; beat at high speed of an electric mixer until stiff peaks form. Fold chopped candies into sweetened whipped cream.

Place one cake layer on a serving plate; spread ¼ cup whipped cream mixture on cake layer. Repeat procedure with remaining cake layers, spreading ¼ cup whipped cream mixture between each layer. Frost top and sides of torte with remaining whipped cream mixture. Cover and chill or freeze until ready to serve or up to 8 hours.

Pull a vegetable peeler down sides of reserved 8 candies to make tiny shavings. Sprinkle candy shavings over torte before serving. **Yield:** one 9" torte.

Note: For fat-free chocolate pound cake, we used Entenmann's.

Chocolate Mint Torte

Caramel-Walnut Brownies

Caramel-Walnut Brownies

These brownies are so luscious and gooey, you'll want to refrigerate them—or plan to eat them with a fork!

   1 (14-ounce) package caramels
⅔ cup evaporated milk, divided
   1 (18.25-ounce) package caramel-flavored cake
      mix
¾ cup butter or margarine, melted
   2 teaspoons vanilla extract
¾ teaspoon ground cinnamon
1½ cups walnut halves or pieces

Unwrap caramels, and place in a medium saucepan. Add ⅓ cup evaporated milk; cook over low heat until caramels melt, stirring often. Remove from heat, and set aside.

Combine remaining ⅓ cup milk, cake mix, and next 3 ingredients; stir just until blended. Spread half of dough into a lightly greased 9" square pan. (Remaining dough will stiffen as it sits.) Bake at 350° for 10 minutes. Cool in pan on a wire rack 5 minutes.

Pour caramel mixture over brownie layer in pan. Sprinkle with walnuts.

Divide remaining half of dough into 6 portions. Shape each portion into a 4" circle. Place circles over walnuts in pan, overlapping slightly. (Dough will spread during baking.)

Bake at 350° for 25 minutes. Cool completely in pan on wire rack. Cover and chill thoroughly before cutting. **Yield:** 15 brownies.

Note: For caramel-flavored cake mix, we used Duncan Hines.

Coffee Crunch Pie

We recommend using Pecan Sandies in this crust. And if you're not a fan of coffee ice cream, vanilla makes a fine filling substitute.

2¼ cups pecan shortbread cookie crumbs
  ¼ cup plus 2 tablespoons butter or margarine, melted
  1 cup coarsely crushed English toffee-flavored candy bars
  1 quart coffee ice cream, slightly softened
  1 (16-ounce) can coconut-pecan frosting
    Garnishes: frozen whipped topping (thawed), flaked coconut, pecans

Combine shortbread cookie crumbs and butter; press firmly in bottom of a greased 9" springform pan. Bake at 350° for 8 to 10 minutes or just until toasted. Sprinkle crushed toffee bars over crust while crust is still warm. Cool completely.

Spread coffee ice cream over candy. Cover and freeze 30 minutes or until firm. Spread coconut-pecan frosting over ice cream. Cover and freeze several hours or until firm.

Remove pie from freezer, and let stand 5 minutes at room temperature. Remove sides of pan before serving. Garnish, if desired. **Yield:** one 9" pie.

Coffee Crunch Pie

Frozen Toffee Log

Frozen Toffee Logs

Make this dessert by sandwiching a whipped topping mixture between crisp cookies—it's a little like putting mortar between bricks.

  1 (7.5-ounce) package almond brickle chips, divided
  1 (12-ounce) container frozen whipped topping, thawed
  1 (9.5-ounce) package brown edge wafer cookies
  ¼ cup caramel topping

Reserve ¼ cup almond brickle chips. Fold remaining brickle chips into whipped topping. Reserve 1¾ cups whipped topping mixture in refrigerator.

Stack 6 cookies, spreading 1 rounded tablespoon of the remaining whipped topping mixture between each cookie. Repeat procedure until 8 stacks of 6 cookies each are formed.

Lay 4 cookie stacks on their sides on a large serving plate, one stack at a time. Spread 1 rounded tablespoon whipped topping mixture between each stack, and gently press stacks together to form a log about 9" long. Repeat procedure with remaining 4 cookie stacks. Cover and freeze logs on plate 15 minutes.

Frost logs with reserved 1¾ cups whipped topping mixture. Sprinkle with reserved ¼ cup brickle chips. Cover loosely, and freeze logs several hours.

Stir caramel topping well; drizzle over logs just before serving. **Yield:** 10 servings.

Note: You can substitute 1⅓ cups finely crushed English toffee-flavored candy bars for the almond brickle chips.

Sugar Cookie Ice Cream Sandwiches

Peppermint ice cream should be easy to find during the holiday season. If it's not available, stir 1 cup crushed hard peppermint candies into 1½ quarts softened vanilla ice cream.

1½ quarts peppermint ice cream, slightly
    softened
1 (20-ounce) package refrigerated sliceable
    sugar cookie dough
⅓ cup hot fudge topping
    Hard peppermint candy, coarsely crushed, or
    multicolored decorator sprinkles

Spread softened ice cream evenly into two wax paper-lined, 8" round cakepans; cover and freeze until ice cream is firm.

Slice cookie dough into 16 (½"-thick) slices. Place 3" apart on lightly greased cookie sheets.

Flatten each cookie to a 2" circle. Bake at 350° for 8 minutes. (Cookies will spread during baking.) Cool on cookie sheets 1 minute. Remove to wire racks, and cool completely. Spread 1 teaspoon fudge topping on bottom of each cookie.

Remove ice cream from pans, working quickly with one pan at a time; peel off wax paper. Cut ice cream into 3" circles, using a 3" biscuit cutter. Place each ice cream circle between 2 cookies, fudge sides in; press gently. Place sandwiches in freezer on a cookie sheet. Cover and freeze 30 minutes.

Roll sides of each ice cream sandwich in crushed peppermint candy or decorator sprinkles. Serve sandwiches immediately, or wrap each sandwich in plastic wrap and freeze. **Yield:** 8 sandwiches.

Sugar Cookie Ice
Cream Sandwiches

Peanut Butter
Brownie Trifle

Peanut Butter Brownie Trifle

Peanut butter and chocolate fanatics will think heaven dwells in this dessert. Any type of brownie mix will work fine here—only the color of the brownie layers will change.

  1 (21.4-ounce) package deluxe peanut butter
    brownie mix or chocolate-peanut butter
    brownie mix
  1 (5.1-ounce) package vanilla instant pudding
    mix
  3 cups milk
  ½ cup creamy peanut butter
  2 teaspoons vanilla extract
  1 cup whipping cream, whipped and divided
  2½ cups coarsely chopped peanut butter cup
    candies, divided
    Garnish: additional peanut butter cup
    candies, sliced

Line a 13" x 9" x 2" pan with a large sheet of aluminum foil, allowing foil to extend 2" out of both ends of dish.

  Prepare brownie mix according to package directions, using packets included in package. Bake according to package directions in prepared pan. Cool completely.

  Lift foil out of pan. Invert brownies onto a cutting board; remove foil. Cut brownies into ¾" pieces, using a sharp knife.

  Combine vanilla pudding mix and milk in a large mixing bowl; beat at low speed of an electric mixer 2 minutes or until thickened. Add peanut butter and vanilla; beat until smooth. Gently fold in half of whipped cream. Set remaining whipped cream aside (about 1 cup).

  Place half of brownies in bottom of a 3-quart trifle bowl; top with 1¼ cups chopped peanut butter cup candies and half of pudding. Repeat layers with remaining half of brownies, 1¼ cups peanut butter cup candies, and pudding. Pipe or spoon reserved whipped cream over trifle. Garnish, if desired. **Yield**: 12 servings.

Easy Chocolate Chewies

This is the easiest chocolate cookie recipe around. Its top takes on a crackled appearance during baking.

  1 (18.25-ounce) package devil's food cake mix
  ½ cup vegetable shortening
  2 large eggs, lightly beaten
  1 tablespoon water
  ½ cup sifted powdered sugar

Combine first 4 ingredients in a large bowl, stirring until smooth.

  Shape dough into 1" balls; roll in powdered sugar. Place balls 2" apart on lightly greased cookie sheets.

  Bake at 375° for 10 minutes. Cool about 10 minutes on cookie sheets. Remove to wire racks to cool completely. **Yield**: 4 dozen.

Dressed-Up Desserts in No Time

Want an easy idea for last-minute holiday desserts? You can make spontaneous hospitality your strong suit with these basic ingredients that secure instant success.

All you need is:
• Frozen pound cake
• Refrigerated sliceable cookie dough
• Box of favorite brownie mix, cake mix, or
    pudding mix
• Jar of maraschino cherries with stems
• Carton of favorite ice cream or frozen yogurt
• Container of frozen whipped topping
• Flavored syrups or ice cream toppings
• Toasted nuts and flaked coconut
• Favorite candy bars or Christmas candies
    like peppermints
• Chopped fresh fruit or dried fruit

Mimic the layered dessert ideas you get from recipes in this chapter, using convenience products as a jump start. Choose a base, filling, and toppings from the list above to create your own signature dessert.

TASTEFUL CENTERPIECES

Stellar centerpieces await your arrival
on the following pages. Feast your eyes
first; then dig in.

Savory
Cocktail
Tree

White
Chocolate
Star Package

White Chocolate Star Package

With our explicit instructions, you'll find this tempting parcel as straightforward to make as it is dazzling to look at. Once you have the technique down pat, the freehand lacy stars are easy; hearts or circles would work well with the same approach.

> 2 (14- or 16-ounce) packages vanilla-flavored
>   candy drops
>   Wooden skewers
>   Cardboard box
> 2 to 3 Styrofoam blocks
>   Decorative tissue paper and ribbon

Place one package of candy drops in top of a double boiler over hot, not simmering, water. Heat until candy melts, stirring often. Remove from heat; let stand 5 minutes.

For Lacy White Chocolate Stars, draw or trace stars of various sizes (3" to 5" work well) on several sheets of wax paper. Turn paper over, and place on baking sheets.

Spoon about 1 cup melted candy into a heavy-duty, zip-top plastic bag. (Keep remaining melted candy warm over hot water.) Seal plastic bag. Snip a tiny hole in one corner of zip-top bag, using scissors.

Drizzle melted candy over outline of stars on wax paper; then drizzle candy in a lacy design to fill in each star. Let harden slightly, and then drizzle another layer of the lacy design on each star. Chill lacy stars at least 15 minutes or until hardened. Carefully peel hardened stars from wax paper, and turn over.

Pipe or spoon a small dot of melted candy onto the back of each lacy star; press the end of a wooden skewer gently into each lacy star, allowing the dot of melted candy to act as "glue." (Be sure about 2" of skewer is anchored onto each star for stability.) Continue to drizzle additional melted candy to cover the 2" portion of each skewer on back of each star.

Repeat whole procedure with remaining melted candy in top of double boiler.

For Solid Stars, melt remaining package of candy drops in top of double boiler according to procedure used for first package of candy. Draw an 8" x 9" rectangle on a sheet of wax paper. Turn paper over, and place on a baking sheet. Spread melted candy evenly to fill out dimensions of rectangle (about ¼" thick). Let stand at room temperature 35 minutes until almost firm.

Cut out stars or other shapes, using a sharp-edged cookie cutter and applying gentle pressure with fingers to penetrate hardened candy and to help remove candy from tips of cutter. (This procedure is a little tedious. You can dip the cookie cutter in hot water and wipe it dry; then press the warm cutter immediately into the almost firm candy and release candy from cutter very carefully.) Attach skewers to backs of solid stars, using remaining melted candy as "glue" according to procedure used for lacy stars.

For Snowflakes, "glue" 2 stars together, using a small amount of melted candy and a wooden skewer between stars.

For Centerpiece Package Assembly, remove top of an 8" x 8" x 8½" cardboard box. To keep the centerpiece box sturdy, place a brick or other flat, heavy object in bottom of box. Cut 2 to 3 blocks of Styrofoam to fit box opening. Stack Styrofoam on top of brick, filling the box.

Cover box with tissue paper, bunching tissue at the top. (You may have to tape several sheets of tissue paper together to cover box entirely.) Scrunch tissue together loosely at the top with a ribbon bow, leaving enough space at the top to insert white chocolate stars and snowflakes.

Insert as many white chocolate stars and snowflakes as desired into Styrofoam in box through tissue opening. Surround centerpiece with additional tiny packages wrapped in tissue. **Yield:** *27* (3" to 5") white chocolate stars and snowflakes.

Lacy White Chocolate Stars

Terra-Cotta Table Bread

"Breaking bread together" gains new meaning when you center a meal around these rustic pots and loaves. Dinner guests can enjoy literally tearing bread from the centerpiece and dipping it into a little olive oil or a hearty bowl of stew.

  Assorted new terra-cotta pots
  Parchment paper
  Vegetable cooking spray
5 **(32-ounce) packages frozen bread dough,**
  thawed in refrigerator
1 **egg white**
1 **tablespoon water**
  Toppings: all-purpose flour, caraway seeds,
  fennel seeds, poppy seeds, regular oats,
  sesame seeds

Wash terra-cotta pots thoroughly in hot soapy water or in dishwasher; let dry completely.

Trace the bottom of each pot onto parchment paper; cut out each shape, and place paper in bottom of each pot.

Coat insides of pots with cooking spray just before placing dough in each pot. (Pots will absorb cooking spray if left unused for any length of time.)

Place a portion of bread dough (large enough to fill pot half full) in each pot. (Work with one package of dough at a time, keeping remaining dough in refrigerator.) Coat tops of bread dough in pots with cooking spray.

Place pots, uncovered, on bottom rack of a cold oven. (For easy transport of smallest pots, group them together on a baking sheet for rising and baking.) Place a small pan of boiling water in oven. Close oven door, and let bread rise until doubled in bulk. (Rising times will vary based on size of pot. See note at right.)

Remove pots of bread and pan of water from oven. Combine egg white and water; brush egg white mixture evenly over tops of loaves. Sprinkle loaves with desired toppings.

Bake pots of bread at 375° on bottom rack of oven until golden. (See chart at right for baking times.) Cool on wire racks. Run a sharp knife around edge of each loaf to loosen bread from pan.

Terra-Cotta Table Bread

Arrange assorted pots of bread on table, using a chenille throw or a piece of burlap as a table runner. Stack a few pots of bread on top of empty pots that have been turned upside down. Complete the centerpiece by adding seasonal fruit like kumquats, large branches of rosemary or greenery, and shafts of wheat tied with raffia. **Yield:** one bread centerpiece.

Note: For our centerpiece, we used 5 packages of frozen bread dough and a combination of the terra-cotta pots listed in the chart at right. You may wish to use different sizes and numbers of pots—just remember to fill each pot half full with bread dough and to watch closely the rising and baking time of each.

Terra-Cotta Bread Basics
(We measured our pots in diameter from inside top rims.)

Pot Size	Amount of Dough	Rising Time	Baking Time
1 (9½" x 4½" x 5") planter (a huge loafpan!)	2 loaves	about 1 hour and 15 minutes	40 minutes
1 (8") round base	2 loaves	30 minutes	35 to 40 minutes
1 (6") pot	1 loaf	20 minutes	30 minutes
3 (4½") pots	¾ loaf per pot	20 minutes	30 minutes
7 (3") pots	about ¼ loaf per pot	15 to 20 minutes	20 to 25 minutes
6 (2") pots	1 (1½") ball per pot	15 to 20 minutes	20 to 25 minutes

Savory Cocktail Tree

Savory Cocktail Tree

Rows of pimiento cheese balls, colossal olives, and wheat crackers create this one-stop hors d'oeuvre tree. All you need to enhance it is a glass of Chardonnay.

1 small onion, minced
1 clove garlic, minced
1 tablespoon butter or margarine, melted
¼ cup dry white wine
3 cups (12 ounces) finely shredded sharp Cheddar cheese
1 (8-ounce) package cream cheese
1 (3-ounce) package cream cheese
1 (4-ounce) jar diced pimiento, drained well
   Coatings: chopped fresh parsley, finely chopped toasted pecans
1 (12") Styrofoam cone
2 (8-ounce) tubs cream cheese, softened
   Chopped fresh parsley
1 (10-ounce) package baked bite-size whole wheat snack crackers
2 (7-ounce) jars large pimiento-stuffed olives, drained
1 large sweet red pepper, cut in half lengthwise

Cook onion and garlic in butter in a medium skillet over medium-high heat, stirring constantly, until tender. Add wine. Bring to a boil; reduce heat, and simmer, uncovered, until liquid has evaporated. Set aside.

Attach circular rows of crackers, cheese balls, and olives to the frosted cone. Once you've built the first three layers, the task gets easier.

Position knife blade in food processor bowl; add shredded Cheddar cheese and 2 packages (11 ounces) cream cheese. Process until cheeses form a ball, stopping once to scrape down sides. Remove mixture to a medium bowl. Stir in onion mixture and pimiento. Cover and chill at least 30 minutes.

Shape mixture into ¾" balls. Place cheese balls on a wax paper-lined jellyroll pan. Cover and chill at least 8 hours.

Roll half of chilled balls in parsley and half in pecans. Cover and chill until firm.

Wrap plastic wrap around Styrofoam cone, sealing completely. Spread softened tub cream cheese over plastic wrap-coated cone, covering cone completely and making a ½"-thick layer. Sprinkle coated cone with chopped parsley.

Press a circular row of crackers into the cream cheese-coated cone at the base. Attach a circular row of cheese balls at base of cone just above cracker layer, using wooden picks. Attach a circular row of olives above row of cheese balls, using wooden picks. Gently press another row of crackers into the cream cheese-coated cone, creating a shingled effect. Repeat procedure, working in circular rows and covering cone completely.

Cut a large star shape out of each pepper half, using a sharp knife. Secure with a wooden pick at top of tree. Serve remaining cheese balls on crackers around base of tree. **Yield:** 7 dozen cheese balls.

Note: For bite-size whole wheat snack crackers, we used Wheat Thins. For candles, see Sources on page 154.

Vanilla
Foaming Bath
Oil

Scented Dusting
Powder

CHRISTMAS PRESENTS

A gift that will pamper, this
luxurious bath oil and powder set
is made of simple ingredients.
We tell you how to make it and
much more in this chapter. From
fuzzy fleece mittens to ornaments
embroidered with silk ribbon,
these presents are delightful to
make and to give.

Sweet-Scented Gift Set

The fresh fragrance of vanilla graces these lavish toiletries, whose luxury belies the fact that they are made of ingredients from your kitchen. To showcase the bath oil and the silky dusting powder, enhance a plain bottle and a box with ribbon.

Scented Dusting Powder

You will need:
½ teaspoon vanilla extract
1 teaspoon almond oil (or any light oil)
1 cup cornstarch
blender
container with lid

Ribbon-Covered
Powder Box

1. To mix, stir together extract and almond oil. Place cornstarch in blender. With blender setting at low speed, slowly add oil mixture to cornstarch. When well mixed, pour into clean container. (Decorative tins or recycled spice jars with perforated tops make ideal containers.)

2. To use, apply to skin with shaker-type container or use powder puff or brush.
Yield: 8 ounces.

Ribbon-Covered Powder Box

Wrap a small box with ribbon to make a perfect powder box. **To cover the box bottom,** select a ribbon that is wide enough to cover the sides. Wrap the ribbon around the box, folding the ribbon ends under for a neat edge. Secure the ribbon ends and edges to the box with craft glue.

To cover the box lid, glue the ribbon around the sides and to the top. Crisscross 2 lengths of ribbon on the top of the lid, gluing the ends to secure. Using thread, gather where the lengths cross. With a short length of ribbon, make a bow. Glue the bow to the center of the box lid. Glue a pearl button to the center of the bow.

Vanilla Foaming Bath Oil

You will need:
1 cup light vegetable oil
½ cup glycerin
½ cup mild liquid soap
1 tablespoon vanilla extract
container with tight-fitting lid

1. **To mix,** stir together all ingredients until well blended. Pour into clean, dry container and close with tight-fitting lid or stopper.

2. **To use,** shake well to reblend ingredients. Pour ¼ cup under running water when filling bath. **Yield:** 16 ounces.

Ribbon-Covered Bottle

Note: For mesh ribbon, see Sources on page 154.

Use 2 lengths of gold mesh ribbon to turn a plain square bottle into an elegant bath oil container. **To cover the bottle,** cut each ribbon length long enough to go down 1 side of the bottle, under the bottom, and up the other side, plus 2". Lay 1 ribbon length over the other at the center, forming a cross. Baste the ribbons together at the center. Place the bottle in the center of the crossed ribbons. Pull the ribbon lengths up to cover the sides of the bottle. Using narrow cording, whipstitch the ribbon edges together, working through holes in the mesh. Begin at 1 top corner of the bottle and stitch along the bottom, ending at the opposite top corner of the bottle. Repeat for the other side. Knot the cording at the top of the ribbon. Remove the basting stitches at the center of the ribbons.
   To secure the ribbon, wrap gold thread tightly around the bottle neck. Attach decorative beads at the corners of the ribbon if desired. Wrap the cording around the cork and glue to secure.

Ribbon-Covered Bottle

Swirling Ribbon
Stocking

Cheery Christmas Cover-up

STIR UP A LITTLE HOLIDAY SPIRIT WITH this festive appliquéd apron. The stockings press on with Velcro, so your favorite chef can wash the apron with ease.

Swirling Ribbon Stocking

You will need:
pattern on page 146
¼ yard fabric
¼ yard fusible interfacing
2½ yards ⅜"-wide double-sided ribbon to
    coordinate with fabric
Velcro coin fasteners
bib-style apron

Note: All seam allowances are ½". For apron, see Sources on page 154.

1. **To make stocking,** using pattern, cut 1 stocking each from fabric and interfacing. With raw edges aligned, fuse interfacing stocking to wrong side of fabric. Trim all edges ½" and leave them unfinished.

2. **To attach ribbon,** 1¼" down from upper left corner of stocking, secure ribbon to fabric with a few machine stitches. Randomly loop and turn ribbon, securing as needed. Wind and loop ribbon as desired down to stocking toe and then back up near stocking top. Trim excess. Hide cut end under ribbon piece and tack in place.

3. **To make hanger,** cut 5" length of ribbon and fold in half. Tack ends to back of stocking.

4. **To make cuff,** in 1 top corner, attach 1 end of remaining length of ribbon with a few machine stitches. Fold ribbon up and down to create a zigzagged cuff, stitching ribbon at top and bottom points to secure. Hide remaining cut end under ribbon piece and tack in place.

5. **To attach stocking to apron,** stick Velcro coin sets to apron and back of stocking, centering stocking on bib of apron.

Ribbon Ruff Stocking

You will need:
pattern on page 146
¼ yard fabric
¼ yard fusible interfacing
1 yard 1½"-wide ribbon to coordinate with fabric
½ yard ⅜"-wide ribbon to coordinate with fabric
Velcro coin fasteners
bib-style apron

Note: All seam allowances are ½". For apron, see Sources on page 154.

1. **To make stocking,** using pattern, cut 2 stockings from fabric and 1 stocking from interfacing. Fuse interfacing stocking to wrong side of 1 fabric stocking.

2. **To make ribbon ruff,** 1½" from top edge of interfaced piece, mark stitch intervals by placing

Ribbon Ruff Stocking

pins ¼" apart across stocking width, beginning and ending with pins placed ¾" in from raw side edges. With raw edges aligned, machine-stitch 1½"-wide ribbon to stocking at 1 (¾") mark. Fold 1" loop in ribbon and machine-stitch at adjacent ¼" mark. Repeat to stitch ribbon at ¼" intervals, keeping ribbon 1½" from stocking top. Machine-stitch last loop at remaining ¾" mark. Trim ends evenly.

3. **To add heel and toe accents,** referring to pattern, cut lengths of ⅜"-wide ribbon and baste to stocking heel and toe.

4. **To make hanger,** cut 5" length of ⅜"-wide ribbon and fold in half. With raw edges aligned, baste ends to right side of stocking in top right corner, ½" in from side.

5. **To stitch pieces together,** with right sides facing and raw edges aligned, machine-stitch stockings together, leaving 3" opening at top. Be sure not to catch ribbon loops in stitching. Trim seams, clip curves, turn, and press. Slipstitch opening closed.

6. **To attach stocking to apron,** stick Velcro coin sets to apron and back of stocking, centering stocking on bib of apron.

Silk Ribbon Bouquets

Embroidery stitches bloom in bouquets destined to be cherished. To fashion a brooch, attach a pin back. Or make an ornament by adding a simple ribbon loop.

Round Ornament

You will need:
diagrams on pages 148-149
1 sheet each felt: burgundy, antique white, hunter green
1"-diameter round crocheted flower medallion
size 20 chenille needle
4-mm silk ribbon: (146) dark rose pink, (128) medium rose pink, (111) light pink, (20) medium green (Numbers correspond to YLI silk ribbon.)
2-mm gold ribbon thread
4-mm gold ribbon for bow and hanger

Note: For ribbon and felt, see Sources on page 154.

1. To embroider flowers, using diagram, trace designated circle onto burgundy felt and cut out. Tack crocheted flower medallion to center of burgundy felt circle. Follow diagram to stitch flowers.

2. To make ornament, using diagram, trace designated circle onto antique white felt and cut out. Center burgundy felt circle on antique white circle. Using blanket stitch and gold thread, sew burgundy and antique white circles together, leaving small opening. Stuff with cotton balls. Slipstitch opening closed. Sew edge of antique white felt with overcast stitch, pulling stitches tight to form scallops. Tack to green felt. Trim green felt along edge of antique white felt, leaving about ⅛" green border.

3. To make hanger, use 6" length of 4-mm gold ribbon to make hanger loop. Tie ends together to form bow.

Heart Pin

You will need:
diagrams on pages 148-149
purchased crocheted heart medallion (approximately 1¾" x 2")
1 sheet each felt: sage green, burgundy
size 20 chenille needle
4-mm silk ribbon: (128) medium rose pink, (111) light pink, (84) dark purple, (20) medium green (Numbers correspond to YLI silk ribbon.)
cotton balls
pin back

1. To embroider flowers, cut sage green felt into 5" square. Tack crocheted heart medallion in center of square. Follow diagram to stitch flower spray.

2. To make pin, trim green felt along edge of crocheted heart. Tack to burgundy felt, leaving small opening. Trim burgundy felt around heart. Stuff with cotton balls. Slipstitch opening closed. Sew pin back in place on back of heart.

Julie McGuffee of Fort Worth, Texas, especially enjoyed designing these projects for us since, as she said, "Working with felt brought back childhood memories of sitting in front of a roaring fire, stitching felt ornaments for the family tree."

Heart Pin

Round Ornament

Heart Ornament

Heart Ornament

You will need:
diagrams on pages 148-149
1 sheet each felt: antique white, burgundy
size 20 chenille needle
4-mm silk ribbon: (175) dark rose, (104) medium pink, (177) medium purple, (72) dark green, (54) gold (Numbers correspond to YLI silk ribbon.)
cotton balls
pearls by the yard

1. To embroider flowers, using diagram, trace heart pattern onto antique white felt and stitch.

2. To make ornament, cut out heart. Center on burgundy felt and sew along edge, leaving small opening. Stuff with cotton balls. Slipstitch opening closed. Using thread, sew pearls along edge of antique white felt. Using pinking shears, trim burgundy felt along edge of antique white felt, leaving about ⅜" burgundy border.

3. To make hanger, use 6" length of dark rose ribbon to make loop. Attach at center top of heart.

Christmas Bough Stationery & Picture Mat

Gift Tag

Picture Mat

Invitation

YOU CAN USE THIS ORIGINAL ARTWORK to make a mat for a photo, a party invitation, or a gift tag. All you have to do is duplicate the image on a color copier (available at copy centers). We used card stock for a more substantial feel.

Tennessee artist **Susan Harrison** created this artwork especially for ***Christmas with Southern Living***. You'll appreciate the many ways to use it during the season. Whether for the ideas pictured here, calling cards, or Christmas photo cards—you'll have a custom-designed look at a fraction of the cost of retail.

To make the mat, copy the image at 100%. Trim the outer and inner edges to fit in a 5" x 7" acrylic frame. Position the photo behind the mat. Tape the photo in place. Insert the photo and the mat into the frame.

To make the invitation or the gift tag, copy the image larger, smaller, or same size, according to the approximate desired size. Trim the outer edges.

Note: Artwork is copyright free.

Bright and Fleecy Winter Warmers

Fanciful fringed edges and contrasting colors fashion a scarf-and-mittens set for the young or the young at heart.

Mittens

Polar Fleece Scarf

You will need:
½ yard each 60"-wide polar fleece: purple, red
buttonhole twist: purple, red (optional)
pinking shears

Note: For polar fleece, see Sources on page 154.

1. To cut out scarf, cut 1 (13" x 60") piece each from purple and red fleece. Trim selvages.

2. To make scarf, with edges aligned, pin pieces together. Trim to match if necessary. Thread machine and bobbin with red thread or, if you prefer stitches to show, thread machine with purple buttonhole twist and bobbin with red buttonhole twist. Set machine for basting stitch. With red fleece side up, stitch pieces together, using 1" seam allowance on sides and 4" seam allowance on ends.

3. To finish edges, using pinking shears, trim ½" from all edges. Clip ½"-wide fringe up to seam line at each end of scarf.

Polar Fleece Mittens

You will need:
diagram on page 144
⅓ yard each 60"-wide polar fleece: purple, red
1 yard ⅞"-wide red single-fold bias tape
½ yard ½"-wide nonroll elastic
pinking shears

Note: For polar fleece, see Sources on page 154.

1. To make mitten pattern, lay 1 hand on blank sheet of paper, slightly extending thumb and keeping fingers close together. With pencil, mark both sides of wrist bone on paper. Holding pencil straight up, outline shape of entire hand.

Lift hand from paper. For elastic casing markings, draw 1 straight line connecting wrist bone markings and 1 parallel line ½" below. For bottom edge of mitten, draw parallel line 3" below casing markings. Extend side lines of outline to meet bottom of mitten. For cutting line, draw line 1" (¾" for child) from hand tracing around all sides except bottom edge. Cut out pattern.

2. To cut out mittens, position pattern on fleece so that stretch of fabric is across width of mitten. Cut 2 pieces each from purple and red fleece. Lay red pieces on work surface with thumbs pointing toward each other. For each mitten, with edges aligned, pin purple to red piece along edge opposite thumb.

3. To sew each mitten, using ¼" seam allowance, stitch together along pinned edge, starting approximately at tip of small finger and ending 2" from bottom edge (see diagram). Open mitten and measure length of casing. Cut piece of bias tape to this measurement. Center tape between casing lines. Pin tape to mitten, aligning raw ends. Stitch tape to mitten.

4. To insert elastic, measure wrist and add 1½" to measurement. For each mitten, cut piece of elastic to this measurement. Insert elastic through casing and secure at each end.

5. To finish each, refold mitten. Using ¼" seam allowance, continue sewing along edge, ending 2" from opposite bottom edge. Clip all curves. Using pinking shears, pink bottom edges and 2" of side seams. Turn right side out. Fold bottom edge 2" to right side. Stitch ½" from fold.

6. To make trim, using pinking shears, cut ½"-wide fringe up to stitching line on each cuff.

Scarf

Paper Napkin Wraps

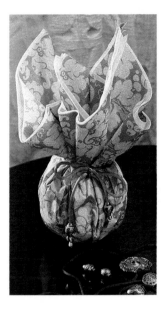

GIFT WRAPPINGS

Cover small packages with printed napkins for style and convenience. On the following pages, we show you some easy ways to wrap: Recycle used shopping bags to make unique gift bags. Create one-of-a-kind tags with stamps. And cover an ordinary box with beautiful fabric.

A small package can pose a big problem. Instead of wrestling with an uncooperative roll of gift wrap, reach for a **paper napkin**. Napkins with holiday motifs are plentiful this time of year, and one will easily wrap a small package. For a fine finish, glue on a tassel or a button. Or pull up the sides and tie them together with a fancy ribbon. For napkins, see Sources on page 154.

Keepsake Boxes

For an important gift or as a
get-organized present to yourself, a fabric-wrapped
container holds promise. The truffle box on our cover is
wrapped with ruby-colored velvet.

You will need:
diagrams on page 147
storage box with removable lid (A variety are
    available at office supply stores. Two 15" x 10"
    x 24" boxes and a 12" x 10" x 15" box were
    used. Do not punch out handle holes.)
fabric: 1¾ yards for each large box, 1¼ yards for
    each small box (Extra yardage is needed if
    fabric pattern positioning is required.)
spray adhesive
2"-wide grosgrain ribbon: 5½ yards for each large
    box, 4¾ yards for each small box

Note: For fabric and ribbon, see Sources on
page 154.

1. To cut fabric for box, for each large box, cut
39½" x 48¾" rectangle; for each small box, cut
36½" x 39½" rectangle. Cut 10" square from each
corner (see diagrams).

2. To cut fabric for box lid, for each large box
lid, cut 23" x 32½" rectangle; for each small box lid,
cut 19" x 22½" rectangle. Cut 2" square from each
corner (see diagrams). To prevent fraying, serge or
zigzag flap ends or use liquid ravel preventer.

3. To glue fabric to box, referring to diagrams
on page 147, fold fabric as indicated and press
lightly. When gluing fabric to box, work in well-
ventilated area and on large flat surface. Cover
surface and use cardboard or posterboard as shield
to protect area from spray.
  To glue fabric to bottom of box, center box on
wrong side of fabric. Tilt box back and spray
adhesive onto bottom of box. Carefully replace box

on fabric. Turn box over and smooth fabric on box.
Turn box back over, placing bottom side down.
  To glue fabric to sides of box, working on 1 side
at a time and beginning with box ends, spray surface
with adhesive. Wrap 2" pressed flaps of fabric around
corners of box. Repeat to cover other end. Spray
front of box with adhesive. Smooth fabric over
surface, making sure that pressed edge of fabric
flap aligns with corners of box. Repeat to cover back
of box.
  Spray adhesive onto inside edge of box. Fold
fabric flap ends to inside, smoothing fabric for
unwrinkled finish. Glue fabric to lid in same manner.

4. To cut ribbon, for each large box, cut 2 (39")
lengths for box, 2 (25") lengths for lid, and 2 (33")
lengths for bows; for each small box, cut 2 (36")
lengths for box, 2 (21") lengths for lid, and 2 (27")
lengths for bows.
  To attach ribbon to box, measure 5¼" in from
each side of large box lid and 3" in from each side of
small box lid. Lightly mark with pencil. Spray glue
on wrong side of 1 lid ribbon. With outside edge of
ribbon just covering 1 pencil mark, glue ribbon in
place, starting at bottom of lid lip and leaving 4" free
to wrap around bow. Wrap other end of ribbon to
inside of box lid. Repeat with remaining lid ribbon.
  Place lid on box. Mark placement of ribbons on
box. Spray back of each box ribbon and glue into
place, wrapping ends to inside.

5. To make bows, fold each remaining ribbon into
bow and tails. Staple to secure shape. Cut tail ends at
an angle. Spray glue onto last 4" of each lid ribbon.
Wrap 1 glued ribbon end around center of each bow
(see photo).

Smart-Shopper Gift Bags

Recycle those department store shopping bags tucked away in your closet. With a little cutting and pasting, you can create wonderful gift bags that are practically free!

To camouflage store labels, glue illustrations from old Christmas cards or squares of tissue paper over the store names. Cut motifs from wallpaper to pull together a classic look or use stickers, ribbon, and holiday papers to assemble a clever collage. Make coordinating gift tags from the same materials. For a flourish, tie big bows of wired ribbon to the handles and stuff the bags with colorful tissue.

Stamped Santa Sacks

MAKE THESE NO-SEW GIFT BAGS FASTER than you can wrap just one gift with paper! Then custom-print each bag with spirited rubber stamps.

You will need:
burlap or linen (Amount will vary according to size of bag desired.)
cardboard for work surface
fabric paints in desired colors
foam paintbrush
rubber stamps
fabric glue
ribbon, raffia, or twine to tie bags
cardboard square for gift tag (optional)

Note: For stamps, paints, and burlap, see Sources on page 154.

   1. To stamp fabric, cut fabric to desired size. Place right side up on top of cardboard to protect work surface. Be sure fabric is free of wrinkles since surface irregularities affect the way stamps print.

   Using foam paintbrush and desired color of paint, paint surface of 1 stamp, taking care to cover entire surface of design evenly. (You may want to practice stamping on scrap of fabric first.) Press stamp to fabric where desired with enough pressure to transfer image. If image is too pale, you may need more paint. If you have too much paint on stamp, there may be drips. Use paintbrush to clean up any excess paint that accumulates on stamp, especially around edges and indentations. If necessary, wipe paint from margins of stamp using cotton swab. Be sure to clean stamp before stamping with different colors. (To clean stamp, spray with household cleaner and let sit for a minute or two; then wash away remaining paint under warm

water.) After stamping design, allow paint to dry before making bag.

2. To make gift bag, with wrong sides of stamped fabric facing and raw edges aligned, fold fabric in half. Turn 1 side edge under ¼". Overlap remaining side edge. Glue together, aligning raw edges inside bag. Let dry. Turn bottom edge under ¼". Glue edge together, aligning raw edges inside bag. Let dry. Ravel fabric at top if desired. Tie with ribbon, raffia, or twine.

3. To make matching gift tag, simply stamp design on cardboard square, punch hole in top corner, and tie on with ribbon.

Designer **Mary O'Neil** of Nashville, Tennessee, carved a potato stamp and launched a career. The rubber stamps she created for her company, Hot Potatoes Fabric Stamps, add stylish designs to her clever no-sew gift bags.

Pretty Papers

Any gift will be well dressed wearing one of these cards. We decorated plain mailing tags, small cards, and hand-made papers with rubber-stamp designs, dressmaker trimmings, and charms. There's no limit to what you, too, can do with a little imagination and a few choice supplies. For rubber stamps and ink, see Sources on page 154.

Stamped Gift Tags

To make the Christmas tree card, simply fold a sheet of card-weight paper in half widthwise. Then cut 2 rectangles, 1 smaller than the other, from decorative or tissue paper. Glue the rectangles onto the front of the card. Bend gold craft wire into a simple tree shape and wrap crinkle wire around the shape to decorate. Secure the wire tree to the card by punching a small hole in the top sheet of paper and bending the wire ends to the back. For crinkle wire, see Sources on page 154.

To make the charm card, fold a rectangle of handmade paper in half widthwise. Gently tear across the bottom edge of the top half for a deckle-edged effect. Cut 2 rectangles, 1 smaller than the other, from decorative or tissue paper. Fold the larger rectangle around the card and glue it to the card back. Center the smaller rectangle on top of the card and glue in place, sandwiching ribbon tails between the large and small rectangles if desired. Glue an inexpensive charm or a decorative button to the center of the card.

GIFTS FROM THE KITCHEN

Simple recipes and smart packages make
gift giving easy. Mix and match from this
lineup to suit all the tastes on
your gift list.

Snowball Sandwich Cookies

Lemon Cream Bonbons

Sugar Cookie Christmas Ornaments

Sugar and Spice Gorp•Pepper Nuts

Sundance Cornmeal Mix

Italian Cheese Terrine

Wax Paper-Wrapped Boxes

Christmas Cones

Cookie Tube

Painted Cans in a Crate

Southwestern Sacks

Italian Goodie Basket

Snowball
Sandwich
Cookies

Snowball Sandwich Cookies

Package miniature sandwich cookies in clever wax paper-wrapped bakery boxes. You can find the 5" boxes at your local bakery.

> 6 ounces white chocolate, chopped
> 2 (12-ounce) bags wedding cookies

Place white chocolate in top of a double boiler; bring water to a boil. Reduce heat to low; cook until chocolate melts, stirring occasionally. Dip bottoms (flat sides) of half the cookies in white chocolate; press flat sides of remaining cookies against dipped cookies, creating sandwiches. Place on wire racks; let stand until white chocolate filling is firm.

    Divide cookies into 4 portions. Pack each portion in a medium-size zip-top plastic bag. Place each bag in a bakery box. **Yield:** 4 dozen.

Wax Paper-Wrapped Boxes

To make the wax paper-wrapped boxes, crumble and uncrumble a 20" length of wax paper. Press the paper flat. Continue to crumble and uncrumble until paper is soft and pliable. Press the paper flat. Fill a tissue paper-lined bakery box with a package of cookies. Close the box, and wrap it with crumbled wax paper.

To make the bow, cut 8 (3"-wide) strips of wax paper. Crumble and uncrumble the strips. Trim the ends in decorative angles, if desired. Gather the stack of strips in the middle, and tie them securely with a twist tie or ribbon. Tie the stack onto the package with gold string. Fluff the stack by lifting and separating each wax paper strip to make a bow. Attach sequins to the wrapped package, using a glue stick. Glue additional sequins onto the gift tag; attach it to the package. Repeat the procedure to make 4 gift packages.

Lemon Cream Bonbons

> ⅓ cup butter, softened
> 2 tablespoons whipping cream
> ½ teaspoon grated lemon rind
> 1 tablespoon lemon juice
> ¼ teaspoon salt
> 3¾ to 4 cups sifted powdered sugar, divided
> 1 (12-ounce) package semisweet chocolate morsels
> 1½ tablespoons shortening
>   Finely chopped pistachios or almonds, toasted

Combine first 5 ingredients in a large mixing bowl; beat at medium speed of an electric mixer until fluffy. Add 2 cups powdered sugar, mixing well. Stir in enough of remaining powdered sugar to make a stiff dough. Shape into 36 (1") balls; chill until firm.

    Combine chocolate morsels and shortening in top of a double boiler; bring water to a boil. Reduce heat to low; cook until chocolate melts. Dip each ball of candy into chocolate mixture. Roll in chopped nuts. Place on wax paper to cool. Chill until firm. **Yield:** 3 dozen.

Christmas Cones

To make the Christmas cones, cut wrapping paper of your choice into an 11¼" square. Place an 11" square of posterboard on top of the square of wrapping paper. (The wrapping paper will make a uniform border around the edges of the posterboard.) Seal the edges of the papers together, using a glue stick or double-sided tape.

    Fold the top corner of the sealed paper down about 1½" and crease it; then open it flat. Beginning with the corner to your left, roll paper into a slender cone (see photo), making a pointed end out of the corner closest to you; secure it with a glue stick or double-sided tape.

    Wrap individual bonbons in small squares of colored tissue. Fill each cone with 6 wrapped candies. Fill the top with additional tissue paper. Gently depress the pre-folded corner to make a partial lid.

Lemon Cream
Bonbons in
Christmas Cones

Wrap the cone with 1 yard of gold cording, securing the cording with hot glue. Write the name of the recipe or a holiday message on a gold sticker. Peel the backing off the sticker, and attach the sticker to the cone. Attach a gold cording tassel, if desired. Repeat the procedure with remaining materials to make a total of 6 bonbon-filled cones.

Sugar and Spice Gorp

You'll need an extra 12-ounce can for packaging this recipe and filling the gift crate as we've done. Save the extra peanuts in a zip-top bag for snacking.

1 egg white
1 tablespoon butter or margarine, melted
1 (12-ounce) can cocktail peanuts
1⅓ cups sugar
1 tablespoon plus 1 teaspoon ground cinnamon
2 teaspoons ground nutmeg
1 teaspoon ground allspice
   Vegetable cooking spray
½ cup raisins
½ cup coarsely chopped dried apricots
1 cup candy-coated chocolate pieces

Beat egg white at high speed of an electric mixer until stiff peaks form; stir in butter. Add peanuts, tossing to coat. (Save the can and plastic lid.)

Combine sugar and next 3 ingredients in a large zip-top plastic bag. Add ¼ cup butter-coated peanuts to sugar mixture, tossing to coat. Remove sugar-coated peanuts with a slotted spoon to a baking sheet coated with cooking spray. Repeat procedure with remaining sugar mixture and butter-coated peanuts.

Bake at 300° for 20 minutes, stirring after 10 minutes. Let cool.

Combine sugar-coated peanuts, raisins, and remaining ingredients; stir well. **Yield:** 5 cups.

Pepper Nuts

2 (6-ounce) cans whole natural almonds
3 tablespoons butter or margarine
3 tablespoons white wine Worcestershire
   sauce
1 teaspoon salt
1 teaspoon chili powder
½ teaspoon garlic powder
⅛ teaspoon ground white pepper
⅛ teaspoon ground red pepper
⅛ teaspoon black pepper

Place almonds in a medium bowl. (Save the cans and plastic lids.) Melt butter in a small skillet or saucepan. Stir in Worcestershire sauce and next 6 ingredients. Cook 1 minute. Remove from heat, and pour over almonds; stir well. Let stand 30 minutes.

Arrange almonds in a single layer on an ungreased jellyroll pan or baking sheet. Bake at 300° for 35 minutes, stirring often. Cool completely. **Yield:** 2 cups.

Painted Cans in a Crate

To make 1 crate with 4 cans, remove the paper labels from the reserved 4 nut canisters. Wind strips of masking tape around each can to cover the can completely. Sponge-paint yellow acrylic paint onto the masking tape-covered cans. Let dry.

Cut 4 circles from a Christmas print fabric, 1½" to 2" larger in diameter than the plastic canister lids. Fill 2 (6-ounce) cans with Pepper Nuts and 2 (12-ounce) cans with Sugar and Spice Gorp. Place the plastic lid on each can. Cover each lid with a fabric cutout, and secure it with a rubber band. Wind several lengths of jute or ribbon around each can to conceal the rubber band.

Fill the wooden crate with shredded paper or moss. Nestle the decorated cans of nuts in the wooden crate.

Sugar Cookie Christmas Ornaments

These cookies offer you a choice: Either bake them yourself, and give them in a holiday tin; or wrap up the cookie dough and a tube of frosting as pictured, and give both as a do-it-yourself present.

> 1 cup butter, softened
> ¾ cup sugar
> 2 egg yolks
> 2½ cups all-purpose flour
> 1 teaspoon baking powder
> Pinch of salt
> ½ cup green decorator sugar
> Red decorator sugar
> White decorator frosting in tube

Beat butter at medium speed of an electric mixer until creamy. Gradually add ¾ cup sugar, beating well. Add egg yolks, beating well.

Combine flour, baking powder, and salt; add to butter mixture, beating well. Stir in green sugar.

Shape dough into a 2"-diameter, 12"-long roll. Roll in red sugar. Wrap roll in wax paper, and chill until firm. (See instructions following recipe for giving this chilled dough as a gift.)

Unwrap dough, and slice into ¼"-thick slices, using a sharp knife. Place on lightly greased cookie sheets.

Bake at 350° for 8 to 10 minutes. Cool 1 minute on cookie sheets. Transfer to wire racks to cool completely. Decorate as desired with decorator frosting. **Yield:** 3 dozen.

Cookie Tube

To make a cookie tube to give this cookie dough as a gift, cut a paper towel tube lengthwise, using scissors. Insert a roll of chilled cookie dough wrapped in wax paper. Twist the ends of the wax paper. Wrap the tube in red Mylar; tie both ends of the tube with metallic ribbon.

Tear 2 opposite sides of 1 sheet of green construction paper to form rough edges. Using a hole punch, punch holes along the torn edges of the paper. Wrap the paper around the tube, and tape it to secure. Write the recipe title or a holiday message on the paper.

Wrap a tube of white decorator frosting in Mylar. Attach it to the cookie dough roll with ribbon. Include a recipe card with baking directions for the cookies with a reminder to store the dough in the refrigerator.

Gently thread 1 folded bandana through the slits in the sack, and tie a square knot in the front. Fold down the top of the sack in 1" pleats. Write the recipe name on the front of the sack, using a black felt-tip marker. Attach a decorative ornament and dried chili peppers.

Include the recipe for Country Christmas Cornbread or Confetti Fritters. Repeat the procedure with the remaining 2 sacks, other materials, and bags of Sundance Cornmeal Mix.

Country Christmas Cornbread

1 package (2⅔ cups) Sundance Cornmeal Mix
1 cup (4 ounces) shredded sharp Cheddar cheese
1 cup milk
¼ cup butter or margarine, melted
6 slices bacon, cooked and crumbled
2 large eggs, lightly beaten

Combine all ingredients in a large bowl; stir just until blended.

Pour mixture into a greased 8" square pan or 8" cast-iron skillet.

Bake at 400° for 28 to 30 minutes or until golden. **Yield:** 9 servings.

Confetti Fritters

Serve these fritters as a hot appetizer with tartar sauce or as an accompaniment for chili.

1 package (2⅔ cups) Sundance Cornmeal Mix
¾ cup sliced or chopped green olives
1 (7-ounce) can mexicorn, drained
1 (2-ounce) jar diced pimiento, drained
¾ cup boiling water
Vegetable oil

Combine first 4 ingredients in a large bowl; add water, stirring well.

Pour oil to depth of 2 to 3 inches in a Dutch oven or large heavy saucepan; heat to 375°. Carefully drop batter by tablespoonfuls into hot oil. Cook, a few at a time, 1 to 2 minutes or until golden. Drain on paper towels. **Yield:** about 3½ dozen.

Sundance Cornmeal Mix

1 (32-ounce) package self-rising yellow cornmeal mix
1½ cups all-purpose flour
⅓ cup dried onion flakes
¼ cup sugar
1½ tablespoons garlic powder
2 teaspoons ground red pepper
1 teaspoon chili powder
1 teaspoon black pepper

Combine all ingredients in a large bowl, stirring well. Divide mixture into 3 portions (about 2⅔ cups each). Spoon each portion into a zip-top plastic bag; seal each bag securely. **Yield:** about 8 cups.

Southwestern Sacks

To make 3 sacks, cut 2 (2") vertical slits on both sides of a lunch-size brown paper sack, near the top of the sack, using a craft knife. Open the sack, and insert 1 zip-top plastic bag filled with Sundance Cornmeal Mix.

Italian Cheese Terrine

Italian Cheese Terrine

Have provolone cheese and salami thinly sliced at a deli. Packaged, presliced cheese and salami are too thick for this recipe.

  1 pound thinly sliced provolone cheese
  1 (2¾-ounce) jar pesto sauce
  ¾ pound thinly sliced salami
  3 tablespoons commercial Italian salad dressing
    Fresh thyme sprigs (optional)
    Marinara or pasta sauce

Place 1 slice of cheese on a large piece of heavy-duty plastic wrap; spread 1 teaspoon of pesto over cheese. Top with 3 slices of salami. (Do not stack salami.) Brush salami lightly with salad dressing. Repeat layers, using all of cheese, pesto, salami, and salad dressing, and ending with cheese. Surround stack with a few sprigs of thyme, if desired.

Fold plastic wrap over layers, sealing securely. Place a heavy object, such as a small cast-iron skillet, on top of cheese terrine. Cover and chill at least 24 hours or up to 3 days.

Remove plastic wrap to serve terrine. Cut into wedges, using an electric knife or sharp knife. Serve with breadsticks, crackers, and desired sauce.
Yield: one terrine (about 12 appetizer servings).

Italian Goodie Basket

To make the goodie basket, place wrapped Italian Cheese Terrine in a 6" corrugated cardboard box. Wrap a bottle of wine, a large candle, a jar of marinara sauce, and place mats separately in large cloth napkins or pieces of corrugated cardboard; tie each with raffia.

Place all the components in a decorative basket. Tie the basket with ribbon, and attach a gift tag. For corrugated cardboard, see Sources on page 154.

Italian Goodie Basket

Macadamia Pie

White Chocolate
Chunk Fruitcake

NUTTY
DESSERTS

**Rustic Almond-
Pear Tart**

**Bourbon-Pecan
Macaroon Bombe**

These luscious sweets unveil not just one but a variety of shelled treasures. Each dessert celebrates a different nut. You can celebrate the flavors.

White Chocolate Chunk Fruitcake

The wooden pick test won't accurately indicate when this cake is done. Use your fruitcake intuition—the cake is baked when it rises to stand firm in the pan and has a golden crust on top.

1/4 cup butter, softened
1/2 cup firmly packed brown sugar
3 large eggs
1 1/3 cups all-purpose flour
2 teaspoons baking powder
1/4 teaspoon salt
8 ounces white chocolate, chopped
1 cup cashews, coarsely chopped
3/4 cup flaked coconut
1/3 cup candied diced orange peel
1 (3-ounce) package dried cranberries

Grease a 9" x 5" x 3" loafpan; line with wax paper. Grease and flour wax paper. Set aside.

Beat butter at medium speed of an electric mixer until creamy; gradually add brown sugar, beating well. Add eggs, one at a time, beating after each addition.

Combine flour, baking powder, and salt; add to butter mixture, beating at low speed until blended. Fold in white chocolate and remaining ingredients. (Batter will be very chunky and thick.)

Spoon batter into prepared pan. Bake at 300° for 1 hour and 15 minutes. Run a sharp knife around edge of pan to loosen fruitcake; cool in pan on a wire rack 30 minutes. Remove cake from pan; peel off wax paper. Cool completely on wire rack. **Yield:** one 9" fruitcake.

Macadamia Pie

Salted macadamia nuts work fine in this pie. No rinsing is necessary; just pop open the jar, and stir them in.

1 (15-ounce) package refrigerated piecrusts
4 large eggs, lightly beaten
1 cup light corn syrup
1/3 cup sugar
3 tablespoons butter or margarine, melted
1 vanilla bean, split lengthwise
2 (3 1/2-ounce) jars or 1 (7-ounce) jar macadamia nuts
1/2 cup flaked coconut
Vanilla ice cream (optional)

Fit 1 piecrust into a 9" pieplate according to package directions. Cut small circles or other desired shapes from remaining piecrust, using small cookie cutters. Arrange cutouts around edge of pieplate, pressing gently; set aside.

Combine eggs and next 3 ingredients in a medium bowl. Scrape vanilla bean seeds into egg mixture; discard vanilla bean pod. Stir mixture well. Stir in macadamia nuts and coconut. Pour filling into prepared piecrust.

Bake at 325° for 40 to 45 minutes or until filling is set. Let cool completely. Serve with small scoops of ice cream, if desired. **Yield:** one 9" pie.

Bourbon-Pecan Macaroon Bombe

For the soft coconut macaroon cookies in this recipe, we used two 13.75-ounce packages of Archway cookies.

4½ cups soft coconut macaroon cookie crumbs
    (about 23 cookies)
¼ cup bourbon
    Vegetable cooking spray
1 (8-ounce) package cream cheese, softened
1 (14-ounce) can sweetened condensed milk
1 (12-ounce) container frozen whipped topping, thawed
1 cup pecan pieces, toasted
    Quick Caramel Sauce

Place cookie crumbs in a large bowl. Drizzle bourbon over crumbs. Toss well, and let crumbs soak 30 minutes.

Coat a 9-cup mold or large mixing bowl with cooking spray, and line with plastic wrap. Press bourbon-soaked cookie crumbs into prepared mold, forming a shell; set aside.

Combine cream cheese and sweetened condensed milk in a bowl; beat at medium speed of an electric mixer until smooth. Fold in whipped topping and pecans. Spoon mixture into cookie shell. Cover and freeze until firm.

Invert frozen bombe onto a chilled serving platter. Place a damp, warm towel around mold. Remove mold, and peel off plastic wrap. Slice bombe into wedges, and serve with Quick Caramel Sauce. **Yield:** 10 to 12 servings.

Quick Caramel Sauce
1 (12-ounce) jar caramel topping
1 tablespoon butter or margarine
2 tablespoons bourbon

Combine caramel topping and butter in a small saucepan. Cook over medium heat until butter melts and sauce is thoroughly heated, stirring often. Remove from heat, and stir in bourbon. Cool sauce slightly. **Yield:** 1 cup.

Rustic Almond-Pear Tart

Rustic Almond-Pear Tart

Don't look for this tart to slice neatly into wedges. As an option, scoop it into wine goblets or bowls, and drizzle with cream.

⅔ cup whole natural almonds
½ cup sugar
1½ tablespoons all-purpose flour
¼ cup butter or margarine, softened
1 large egg
½ (15-ounce) package refrigerated piecrusts
2½ pounds ripe pears, peeled, cored, and coarsely chopped
½ cup sliced almonds
1 tablespoon sugar

Position knife blade in food processor bowl; add whole almonds, ½ cup sugar, and flour. Process until finely ground. Add softened butter and egg. Process until smooth and blended; set aside.

Roll 1 piecrust to a 14" circle on a lightly floured surface. Place in a 9" pieplate, allowing edges to hang over rim of pieplate.

Spread reserved almond mixture in bottom of pastry. Spoon chopped pear over almond mixture. Fold edges of pastry loosely over filling. (Pastry will not cover tart completely.) Sprinkle sliced almonds and 1 tablespoon sugar over filling.

Bake at 350° for 55 minutes or until golden. Cool on a wire rack. **Yield:** one 9" tart.

Frozen Pistachio
Cheesecake

Frozen Pistachio Cheesecake

Two things distinguish this velvety cheesecake: It's frozen, not baked (except for the crust), and it's made without eggs.

    1 cup pistachio nuts
    1 cup brown edge wafer cookie crumbs
    3 tablespoons sugar
 1/3 cup butter or margarine, melted
 2/3 cup whipping cream
   12 ounces white chocolate, finely chopped
    4 (8-ounce) packages cream cheese, softened
 1/2 cup butter or margarine, softened
 2/3 cup sifted powdered sugar
    2 teaspoons vanilla extract
       Garnish: additional pistachio nuts

Position knife blade in food processor bowl; add 1 cup pistachio nuts. Process until chopped. Add wafer cookie crumbs, 3 tablespoons sugar, and melted butter. Pulse 4 or 5 times or until blended.

Press crumb mixture onto bottom and 1½" up sides of a lightly greased 9" springform pan. Bake at 350° for 12 minutes or until lightly browned. Cool completely on a wire rack.

Bring whipping cream to a simmer in a heavy saucepan over medium heat. Remove from heat, and add chopped white chocolate. Let stand 2 to 3 minutes. Stir gently with a rubber spatula until smooth.

Beat cream cheese and softened butter at medium speed of an electric mixer until creamy. Add powdered sugar, and beat until light and fluffy. Add melted white chocolate mixture and vanilla; beat 3 minutes or until very smooth. Pour batter into prepared crust. Cover and freeze until firm or up to 1 week.

Let stand at room temperature about 30 minutes before serving. Remove sides of pan. Garnish cheesecake, if desired. Cut frozen cheesecake with a sharp knife, dipping knife in hot water and wiping it dry between each slice. **Yield:** one 9" cheesecake.

Peanutty Layer Cake

Graham cracker crumbs displace some of the flour in this cake, giving it a slightly coarse texture that drinks in the gooey frosting.

   1 cup butter or margarine, softened
   2 cups sugar
   4 large eggs, separated
   1 teaspoon vanilla extract
   2 cups all-purpose flour
$\frac{3}{4}$ cup graham cracker crumbs
   1 teaspoon baking soda
$\frac{1}{2}$ teaspoon salt
   1 cup buttermilk
     Peanut-Coconut Frosting
$\frac{1}{2}$ cup unsalted dry-roasted peanuts, lightly toasted

Beat butter at medium speed of an electric mixer until creamy; gradually add sugar, beating well. Add egg yolks, one at a time, beating after each addition. Stir in vanilla.

Combine flour, graham cracker crumbs, soda, and salt; add to butter mixture alternately with buttermilk, beginning and ending with flour mixture. Mix at low speed after each addition until blended.

Beat egg whites at high speed until soft peaks form. Gently fold beaten egg whites into batter. Pour batter into 3 greased and floured 9" round cakepans.

Bake at 350° for 20 to 25 minutes or until a wooden pick inserted in center comes out clean. Cool in pans on wire racks 10 minutes; remove from pans, and cool completely on wire racks.

Reserve $1\frac{1}{4}$ cups Peanut-Coconut Frosting. Spread remaining frosting between layers. Stir $\frac{1}{2}$ cup whole peanuts into reserved frosting. Spread on top of cake. **Yield:** one 3-layer cake.

Peanut-Coconut Frosting

$1\frac{1}{3}$ cups sugar
  1 cup evaporated milk
$\frac{2}{3}$ cup butter or margarine
  4 egg yolks, lightly beaten
$1\frac{1}{2}$ cups flaked coconut
  1 cup unsalted dry-roasted peanuts, lightly toasted and chopped
  1 teaspoon vanilla extract

Combine sugar, evaporated milk, butter, and beaten egg yolks in a large saucepan. Cook, stirring constantly, over medium heat 12 minutes or until mixture is thickened and bubbly. Remove from heat.

Stir coconut, chopped peanuts, and vanilla into butter mixture. Cool completely. **Yield:** 4 cups.

Secrets to Layer Cake Success

Baking the Layers
- Use shortening when a cake recipe calls for a "greased pan" unless otherwise specified.
- Don't sift flour before measuring, except for cake flour. Simply stir the flour, spoon it gently into a dry measuring cup, and level the top.
- Stagger cakepans on center rack of a preheated oven. If placed on separate racks, stagger pans so air can circulate.
- Keep oven door closed until minimum baking time has elapsed. Every time you open the oven door, the oven temperature drops 25 to 30 degrees. Use the oven window and light, instead, so you don't risk uneven baking.
- Keep several wire cooling racks on hand. Cakes that cool on a solid surface may become soggy.

Assembling the Cake
- Be sure cake layers are completely cooled before adding filling and frosting, or frosting may melt and slide off the cake.
- Brush loose crumbs from cake layers.
- Place bottom cake layer upside-down on the serving plate. Place top layer right side up.

Frosting the Cake
- Keep frosting just ahead of spatula. Do not backstroke until entire area is frosted, or spatula may drag crumbs into frosting.
- Frost top of cake last.
- Place 3 or 4 strips of wax paper around edges of serving plate to keep plate neat while frosting cake. Position cake on plate, and frost cake. Carefully pull out wax paper strips, and you'll have a clean plate.

P.S. Unfrosted cake layers freeze best. Wrap cooled cake in aluminum foil, and then in plastic wrap. Freeze up to 5 months. Thaw cake layers in wrapping at room temperature.

**Peanutty Layer
Cake**

Walnut
Fudge Pie

Walnut Fudge Pie

This pie is plenty fudgy without the sauce. But with it, our test kitchen graded this dessert *perfect*.

½ cup firmly packed brown sugar
¼ cup all-purpose flour
¼ cup butter or margarine, melted
1 teaspoon vanilla extract
3 large eggs, lightly beaten
1 (12-ounce) package semisweet chocolate morsels, melted
1½ cups walnut halves
½ (15-ounce) package refrigerated piecrusts
Coffee ice cream
Heavenly Fudge Sauce (optional)

Combine first 5 ingredients, stirring until ingredients are blended. Stir in melted chocolate morsels and walnuts.

Fit piecrust into a 9" pieplate according to package directions. Fold edges under, and flute. Spoon filling into piecrust.

Bake at 375° for 30 minutes. Cool completely on a wire rack. Serve with coffee ice cream, and, if desired, Heavenly Fudge Sauce. **Yield:** one 9" pie.

Heavenly Fudge Sauce

1 (12-ounce) package semisweet chocolate morsels
1 tablespoon butter or margarine
½ cup whipping cream
¼ cup strong brewed coffee

Place chocolate morsels and butter in a heavy saucepan. Cook over low heat until chocolate and butter melt, stirring often. Gradually whisk in cream. Cook, stirring constantly, 2 to 3 minutes or until smooth. Remove from heat; stir in coffee. Serve slightly warm. **Yield:** 2 cups.

Note: Scooped into an attractive jar, leftover Heavenly Fudge Sauce makes a great gift for chocolate-lovers. It's good on other desserts, too.

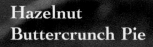

Hazelnut
Buttercrunch Pie

Hazelnut Buttercrunch Pie

Frangelico and a hazelnut praline transform this ice cream pie into an uptown dessert. Place a shot glass of liqueur on each dessert plate, and let guests splash their own servings.

1 cup hazelnuts
1 cup graham cracker crumbs
¼ cup butter or margarine, melted
2 cups vanilla ice cream, slightly softened
1 cup sugar
4 cups chocolate ice cream, slightly softened
Frangelico or other hazelnut-flavored liqueur (optional)

Place hazelnuts in a single layer on an ungreased baking sheet. Bake at 350° for 15 minutes or until skins begin to split. Place hazelnuts in a colander. Rub hazelnuts briskly with a kitchen towel to remove skins; discard skins. Finely chop hazelnuts.

Combine ½ cup chopped hazelnuts, graham cracker crumbs, and butter; stir well. Firmly press mixture evenly in bottom and up sides of a buttered 9" pieplate. Bake at 375° for 7 minutes or until lightly browned. Cool completely on a wire rack.

Spoon softened vanilla ice cream into cooled crust. Cover and freeze until almost firm.

Place sugar in a large heavy skillet. Cook over medium heat, stirring constantly with a wooden spoon, until sugar melts and turns golden (about 20 minutes). Add remaining ½ cup chopped hazelnuts to melted sugar, stirring well. Working rapidly, pour mixture into a 15" x 10" x 1" jellyroll pan lined with aluminum foil; spread in a thin layer. Cool completely. Coarsely break hazelnut praline candy into pieces.

Reserve 1 cup praline candy pieces for garnish. Crush remaining candy pieces. Fold crushed candy into softened chocolate ice cream. Spread chocolate ice cream mixture over vanilla ice cream layer. Cover and freeze at least 8 hours or until firm.

Top each serving with reserved praline candy pieces and, if desired, a splash of Frangelico.
Yield: one 9" pie.

CHRISTMAS DINNER

Please the whole family with this menu
that renews old Southern flavors.

Menu
Serves 8

Sage-Roasted Turkey with
Glazed Carrots

Cranberry-Walnut Dressing

Mashed Potatoes with Sage Butter

Oyster and Onion au Gratin

Green Beans with Country Ham

Frozen Cranberry-Gingersnap Salad

Butternut Spice Pie   Butter-Pecan Cake

This rustic-themed menu debuts what I call "new Old-South cuisine"—innovative twists on recipes true to their Southern roots.

This feast dresses up down-home tastes. Here's how: Fresh sage fills the turkey with flavor, while a bold basting of currant jelly makes the bird glisten. Slivers of crusty country ham add that Southern touch to green beans bathed in a balsamic glaze. Cranberries kiss the menu red as they appear in both the dressing and the salad. And the skins stay on these butter-colored potatoes.

Foods Editor
Julie Fisher

Yes, some things are too traditional to change, but I like a bit of flexibility. The men in my family demand that oysters appear annually on the menu. For them, I make Oyster and Onion au Gratin. Otherwise, the golden-crusted dish is just as good with twice the onions and no oysters.

As for the finale, one dessert offering is fairly simple, the other more involved. You might expect canned pumpkin, but this pie struts butternut squash. And rightfully so, as roasting the squash contributes a caramelized flavor to a filling you won't soon forget. White chocolate yields a tender crumb in the other choice, a slightly elaborate layer cake swirled with a cream cheese frosting. Both desserts deliver a rich finish for a fine meal.

Suggestions for advance preparation come from personal experience, and the prep plan that follows should help your aim for a flawless meal. As for the table setting, my clan doesn't typically count on place cards, yet this year I couldn't resist letting lady apples make the menu—or at least the table. I hope you'll let them beckon your family to this feast.

Julie's Prep Plan

ONE WEEK AHEAD:
• Bake and freeze cake layers of Butter-Pecan Cake.

TWO TO THREE DAYS BEFORE CHRISTMAS:
• Place turkey in refrigerator to thaw, if preparing a frozen bird.
• Prepare and freeze Frozen Cranberry-Gingersnap Salad.
• Prepare and chill Sage Butter.

THE DAY BEFORE CHRISTMAS:
• Thaw cake layers.
• Chop and sauté ingredients for Cranberry-Walnut Dressing. Combine all ingredients except broth and orange juice; cover and chill overnight.

CHRISTMAS MORNING:
• Frost cake.
• Prepare and bake Butternut Spice Pie.
• Toast almonds, and wash and trim green beans for Green Beans with Country Ham.
• Bake Oyster and Onion au Gratin.

THREE HOURS BEFORE THE MEAL:
• Dress turkey, and place in oven to roast.
• Finish preparing dressing. Add dressing to oven during the last hour the turkey roasts.
• Prepare Mashed Potatoes with Sage Butter and Green Beans with Country Ham.

THIRTY MINUTES BEFORE THE MEAL:
• Remove Frozen Cranberry-Gingersnap Salad from freezer to thaw.
• Reheat au gratin.

Sage-Roasted Turkey with Glazed Carrots

    1 (10-pound) turkey
      Salt and pepper
    2 large bunches fresh sage
    ¼ cup butter or margarine, melted and divided
    1 pound carrots, scraped
    1 (10-ounce) jar red currant jelly
    ¼ cup butter or margarine
    1 teaspoon coarsely ground pepper
      Garnish: fresh sage

Remove giblets and neck from turkey; reserve for other uses. Rinse turkey thoroughly with cold water; pat dry. Sprinkle cavity with salt and pepper. Insert 2 bunches fresh sage into body and neck cavities of turkey; tie ends of legs together with string. Lift wingtips up and over back, and tuck under bird.

   Line a roasting pan with heavy-duty aluminum foil; lightly grease foil. Place turkey, breast side up, in prepared pan. Sprinkle turkey generously with salt and pepper; brush with 2 tablespoons melted butter. Insert meat thermometer into meaty portion of thigh, making sure it does not touch bone.

   Bake, uncovered, at 325° for 1½ hours, basting with additional 2 tablespoons melted butter after 45 minutes.

   Cut carrots crosswise into 3" pieces. Cut fatter pieces in half lengthwise.

   Combine jelly, ¼ cup butter, and 1 teaspoon coarsely ground pepper in a small saucepan. Cook over medium heat, stirring constantly, until jelly and butter melt; remove from heat. Brush about one-third of jelly glaze over turkey.

   Arrange carrots around turkey in pan, and brush lightly with jelly glaze. Bake 1 additional hour or until thermometer registers 180°, brushing carrots and turkey with remaining glaze every 15 minutes. Let turkey stand 15 minutes before carving.

   Transfer turkey and carrots to a serving platter, reserving glaze in pan; skim and discard fat from glaze. Place glaze in a medium saucepan; bring to a boil. Cook, uncovered, 8 minutes or until glaze is slightly thickened and reduced by one-third.

   Brush turkey with about ⅓ cup reduced glaze. Pour remaining glaze over carrots. Garnish platter with fresh sage, if desired. **Yield:** 10 servings.

Cranberry-Walnut Dressing

Add sausage to this dressing for a meaty variation. Just brown 1 pound spicy sausage in a skillet, and stir it into the dressing before baking.

    5 cups coarsely crumbled cornbread
    4 cups sourdough bread cubes
    2 cups chopped Vidalia onion or other
      sweet onion
    1 cup sliced celery
    3 cloves garlic, chopped
    ½ cup butter or margarine, melted
    2 (3-ounce) packages dried cranberries
  1½ cups walnut halves, toasted
    2 teaspoons coarsely ground pepper
    2 teaspoons rubbed sage
    ¾ teaspoon ground cinnamon
  1½ to 2½ cups chicken broth
    ½ cup orange juice

Combine cornbread and bread cubes in a large bowl; toss and set aside.

   Cook onion, celery, and garlic in melted butter in a large skillet over medium-high heat, stirring constantly, just until tender.

   Add onion mixture, dried cranberries, and next 4 ingredients to bread mixture; stir well. Add broth and orange juice, stirring until mixture is thoroughly moistened.

   Spoon dressing into a greased 13" x 9" x 2" pan. Bake, uncovered, at 325° for 1 hour or until golden. **Yield:** 10 to 12 servings.

Mashed Potatoes with Sage Butter

A potato masher is the ideal tool to use if you want fluffy spuds.

    ½ cup butter or margarine, softened
    3 tablespoons chopped fresh sage
  3½ pounds Yukon Gold or other buttery
      potatoes, unpeeled
    4 large cloves garlic, halved
    ¼ cup butter or margarine, softened
    1 (3-ounce) package cream cheese, softened
  1¼ cups half-and-half, divided
      Salt and pepper to taste
      Garnish: additional fresh sage

Sage Butter

Combine ½ cup butter and 3 tablespoons sage in a small bowl; stir well. Spoon butter mixture onto a sheet of wax paper. Wrap in wax paper, and chill at least 30 minutes or until slightly firm. Roll butter in wax paper, back and forth, to make a 6" log. Chill up to 2 days.

Place potatoes and garlic in a large saucepan; add water to cover. Bring to a boil; reduce heat, and simmer 20 minutes or until potatoes are tender. Drain, reserving garlic with potatoes.

Combine potatoes, garlic, ¼ cup butter, and cream cheese in a large bowl; mash. Add ¾ cup half-and-half, salt, and pepper; mash. Gradually add enough of remaining ½ cup half-and-half until desired consistency.

Unwrap chilled sage butter, and place on a small serving dish. Garnish, if desired, and serve with potatoes. **Yield:** 8 to 10 servings.

Oyster and Onion au Gratin

  4 slices bacon
  2 medium Vidalia onions, thinly sliced
  2 cups saltine cracker crumbs, divided
  2 (10-ounce) containers fresh Standard
     oysters, drained and divided
  2 cups half-and-half
1½ teaspoons fresh thyme or ½ teaspoon
     dried thyme
  1 teaspoon pepper
¾ cup soft whole wheat breadcrumbs
¼ cup grated Parmesan cheese
  2 tablespoons butter or margarine, melted

Cook bacon in a large Dutch oven over medium heat until crisp; remove bacon, reserving drippings in Dutch oven. Crumble bacon, and set aside. Add onion to drippings in Dutch oven; cook 5 minutes over medium-high heat or until tender. Reduce heat to medium-low; cook 20 minutes or until onion is golden and caramelized, stirring occasionally.

Sprinkle 1 cup cracker crumbs in a lightly greased 2-quart oval baking dish. Top with half each of oysters and onion. Repeat layers with remaining crumbs, oysters, and onion.

Combine half-and-half, thyme, and pepper. Pour mixture over top of casserole. Combine crumbled bacon, breadcrumbs, Parmesan cheese, and melted butter; toss well. Sprinkle over casserole. Bake, uncovered, at 350° for 40 minutes. **Yield:** 8 servings.

Green Beans with Country Ham

  2 pounds fresh green beans
  2 tablespoons olive oil
¼ pound country ham, cut into slivers
  1 medium-size purple onion, thinly sliced
⅓ cup balsamic vinegar
  2 teaspoons sugar
¼ teaspoon pepper
¼ cup sliced natural almonds, toasted

Wash beans, and remove strings, if desired; trim stem ends. Arrange beans in a steamer basket over boiling water. Cover and steam 10 minutes or until crisp-tender.

Heat oil in a cast-iron skillet over medium heat until hot. Add ham and onion, and cook just until onion is tender. Remove ham and onion from skillet with slotted spoon; set aside.

Add vinegar to skillet. Bring to a boil; reduce heat, and simmer, uncovered, 5 minutes or until liquid is reduced by half. Add sugar and pepper, stirring well. Add ham and onion, stirring just until coated. Remove from heat; pour ham mixture over green beans, tossing gently. Sprinkle with almonds. **Yield:** 8 servings.

Frozen Cranberry-Gingersnap Salad

2 cups crushed gingersnap cookies
¼ cup butter or margarine, melted
1 (8-ounce) package cream cheese, softened
1 (16-ounce) can whole-berry cranberry sauce
1 (8-ounce) can crushed pineapple, drained
1 (8-ounce) carton sour cream
1 tablespoon brown sugar
½ cup sour cream

Combine gingersnap crumbs and butter; stir well. Reserve ⅓ cup crumb mixture. Press remaining crumb mixture firmly into a greased 8" square pan.

Beat cream cheese at medium speed of an electric mixer until smooth. Add cranberry sauce and next 3 ingredients; stir until blended. Spoon mixture into prepared crust. Cover and freeze until firm.

Let stand 20 to 25 minutes at room temperature before serving. Cut into squares, and top servings evenly with sour cream and reserved ⅓ cup crumb mixture. **Yield:** 8 servings.

Lady apple place cards will lure guests to the table. To make the place cards, fill miniature gold baskets with moss. Cut slits two-thirds deep through center of each apple; insert small place cards. Perch apples in baskets. For baskets, see Sources on page 154.

Butternut Spice Pie

Ground red pepper is no mistake in this filling—it blends well with the other spices to enhance the flavor of the butternut squash.

½ (15-ounce) package refrigerated piecrust
1 (2-pound) butternut squash
3 tablespoons butter or margarine, melted
1 cup heavy whipping cream
¾ cup firmly packed brown sugar
3 tablespoons maple syrup
1 teaspoon ground cinnamon
½ teaspoon salt
½ teaspoon ground ginger
¼ teaspoon ground allspice
⅛ teaspoon ground red pepper
2 large eggs, lightly beaten
  Sweetened whipped cream
  Ground cinnamon

Roll piecrust to ⅛" thickness on a lightly floured surface. Place crust in a 9" deep-dish pieplate; flute edges, if desired. Cover and freeze while you prepare filling.

Cut butternut squash in half lengthwise. Place squash halves, cut sides up, in a shallow baking dish or pan. Bake, uncovered, at 350° for 50 to 55 minutes or until squash is tender, basting often with butter. Cool slightly.

Remove and discard squash seeds. Remove squash pulp, discarding shells. Mash pulp. Place 2 cups mashed pulp in a large bowl. (Reserve any remaining mashed pulp for another use.)

Add 1 cup whipping cream and next 8 ingredients to mashed squash pulp; stir well with a wire whisk. Pour mixture into prepared pastry shell.

Bake at 350° for 40 to 50 minutes or until set in center. (Shield piecrust with strips of aluminum foil to prevent excessive browning, if necessary). Cool completely.

Garnish with sweetened whipped cream; sprinkle with cinnamon. **Yield:** one 9" deep-dish pie.

Butternut
Spice Pie

Butter-Pecan
Cake

Butter-Pecan Cake

6 ounces white chocolate, chopped
½ cup boiling water
1 cup unsalted butter, softened
1½ cups sugar
4 large eggs, separated
1 teaspoon vanilla extract
1 cup buttermilk
1 teaspoon baking soda
3 cups sifted cake flour
   Butter-Pecan Frosting
   Garnish: toasted pecan halves

Place chocolate in a bowl. Pour boiling water over chocolate; stir until smooth. Set aside, and let cool.

Grease three 9" round cakepans; line with wax paper. Grease and flour wax paper. Set aside.

Beat butter at medium speed of an electric mixer until creamy; gradually add sugar, beating well. Add egg yolks, one at a time, beating after each addition. Stir in white chocolate mixture and vanilla.

Combine buttermilk and soda. Add flour to butter mixture alternately with buttermilk mixture, beginning and ending with flour. Mix at low speed after each addition until blended.

Beat egg whites at high speed until stiff peaks form. Gently fold into batter. Pour batter into prepared pans.

Bake at 350° for 25 minutes or until a wooden pick inserted in center comes out clean. Cool in pans 10 minutes; remove from pans, and cool completely on wire racks.

Spread Butter-Pecan Frosting between layers and on top and sides of cake. Garnish, if desired.
Yield: one 3-layer cake.

Butter-Pecan Frosting

2 tablespoons butter
1¼ cups coarsely chopped pecans
1 (8-ounce) package cream cheese, softened
1 (3-ounce) package cream cheese, softened
½ cup butter, softened
1 (16-ounce) package powdered sugar, sifted
2 teaspoons vanilla extract

Melt 2 tablespoons butter in a large skillet over medium heat. Add pecans; cook, stirring constantly, 10 minutes or until pecans are toasted. Remove from heat. Cool completely.

Beat cream cheeses and ½ cup butter at medium speed of an electric mixer until creamy. Gradually add sugar; beat until light and fluffy. Stir in buttered pecans and vanilla. Cover and chill at least 1 hour.
Yield: 4½ cups.

Setting a Casual Christmas Table

In the pictures on these pages, we've mixed formal serving pieces with casual dinnerware. This relaxing the elegant is not just a trend—it's the easiest, most practical way to set a bountiful table. To recreate this look for yourself, consider these points:

• Take liberties in mixing old, new, rustic, and refined china, silver patterns, and accessory items for the table.
• Show off your collection of favorite Christmas objects or ornaments. Build a centerpiece using the collection.
• Try a sparkling lineup of mismatched wine glasses.
• Use pottery to make your rustic table more handsome. Pottery conveys a country-style warmth that will enliven the Christmas table. Weave in serving pieces of stoneware or bone china in a display of opposites.
• Experiment with a creative napkin presentation. Let the napkin spill from the bowl of the wine glass, or let it gently drape over the edge of the table. In this menu's table setting, we've tied a knot in each napkin.
• Consider serving the meal buffet style; then eat it as a sit-down dinner. Offering the food on the sideboard allows more room on the table for creative place cards, candles, and a seasonal centerpiece.

Patterns

Paper Bag Holly Garlands

**Instructions begin
on page 66.**
Patterns are full size.

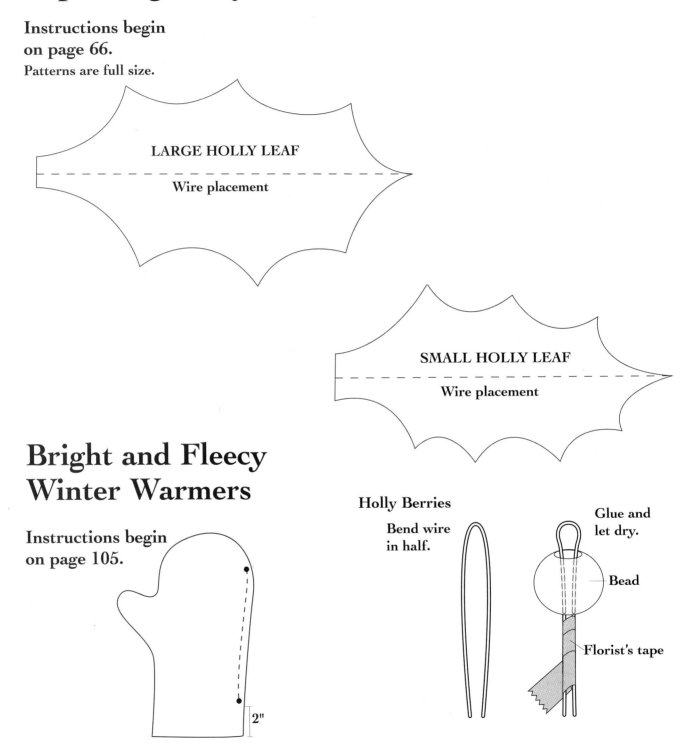

LARGE HOLLY LEAF

Wire placement

SMALL HOLLY LEAF

Wire placement

Bright and Fleecy
Winter Warmers

**Instructions begin
on page 105.**

2"

Holly Berries

Bend wire
in half.

Glue and
let dry.

Bead

Florist's tape

Golden Angel Pillow and Ornament

Instructions begin on page 65.

Pattern is full size.

ANGEL STENCIL

Tree & Holly Tableware

Instructions begin on page 40.

Pattern is full size.

Plate Rim

TREE STENCIL

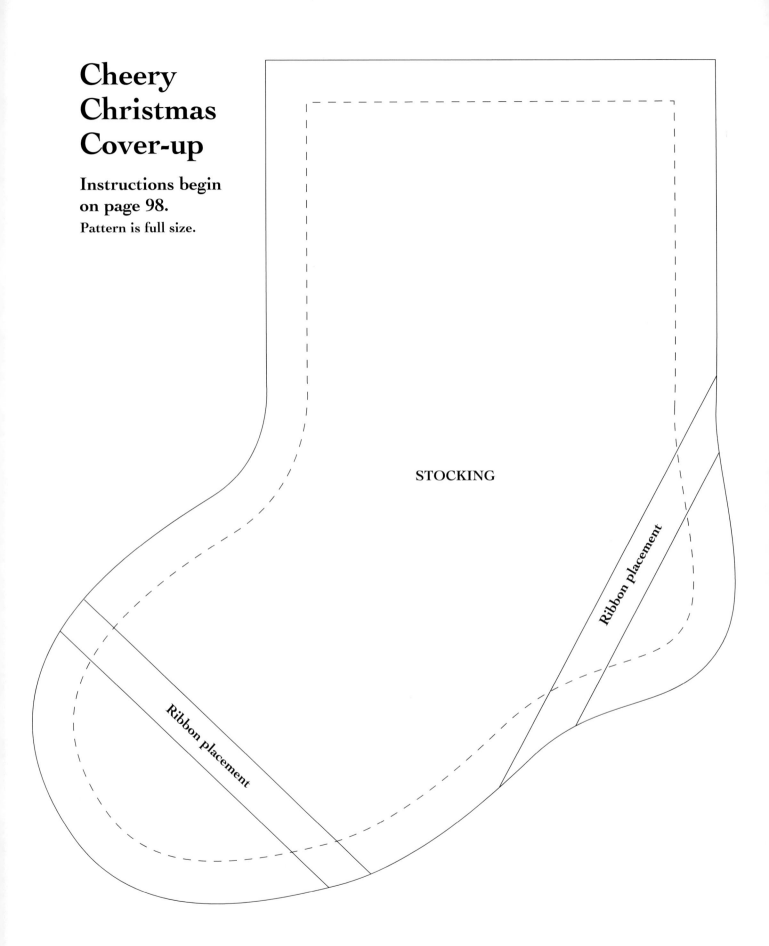

Cheery Christmas Cover-up

Instructions begin on page 98.

Pattern is full size.

STOCKING

Ribbon placement

Ribbon placement

Keepsake Boxes

Instructions begin on page 108.

Fold fabric to wrong side along dotted lines and press lightly.

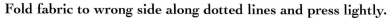

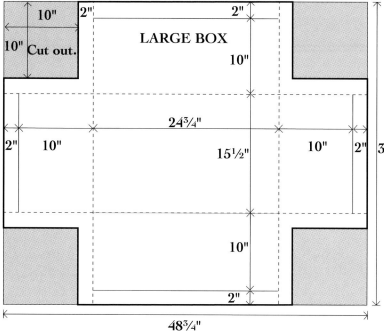

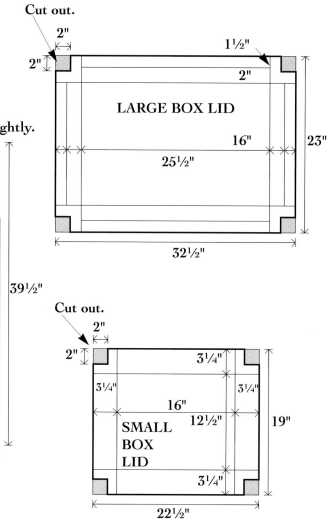

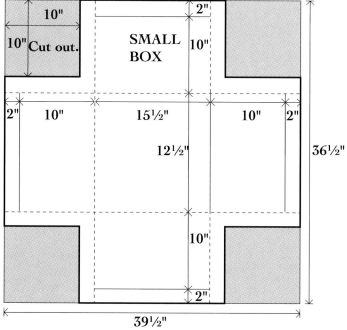

To Cover Different-Sized Boxes:

Using the diagrams as a guide, make a graph following the dimensions of your box. Begin by drawing a box with the measured length and width of your box. Add the height measurement to all 4 sides. Add 2" to all 4 sides for flaps. Total these measurements for the overall rectangle size. The size of each corner cutout is equal to the height measurement. (Example: If the height is 4", cut out a 4" square.) Use the graph to determine the yardage requirements. Measure the box for the ribbon requirements. Each bow will take ¾ yard to 1 yard of ribbon, depending on the size bow desired.

Silk Ribbon Bouquets

Instructions begin on page 100.

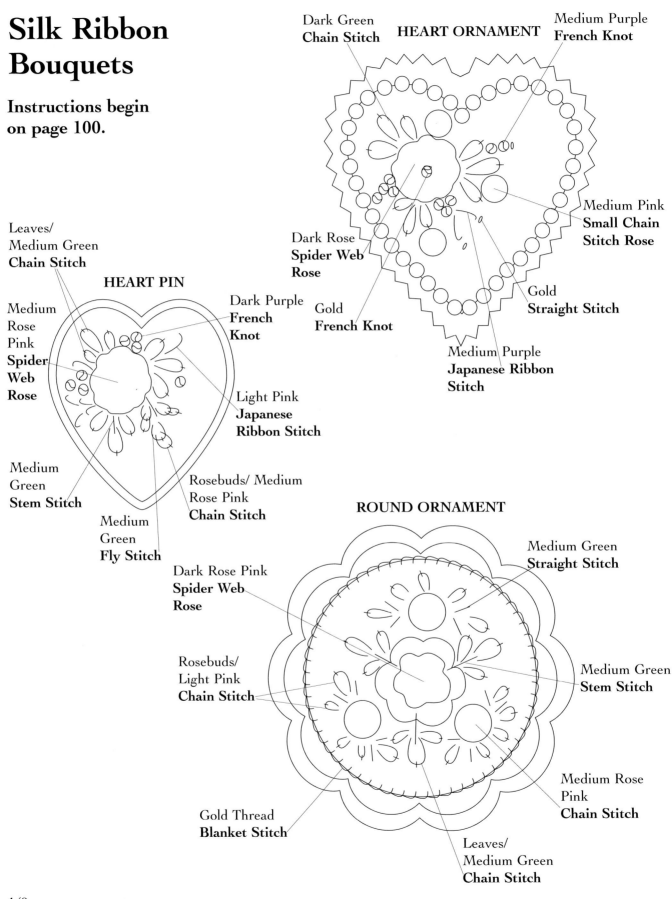

HEART ORNAMENT

Dark Green
Chain Stitch

Medium Purple
French Knot

Medium Pink
**Small Chain
Stitch Rose**

Dark Rose
**Spider Web
Rose**

Gold
Straight Stitch

Gold
French Knot

Medium Purple
**Japanese Ribbon
Stitch**

HEART PIN

Leaves/
Medium Green
Chain Stitch

Medium
Rose
Pink
**Spider
Web
Rose**

Dark Purple
**French
Knot**

Light Pink
**Japanese
Ribbon Stitch**

Medium
Green
Stem Stitch

Medium
Green
Fly Stitch

Rosebuds/ Medium
Rose Pink
Chain Stitch

ROUND ORNAMENT

Dark Rose Pink
**Spider Web
Rose**

Rosebuds/
Light Pink
Chain Stitch

Medium Green
Straight Stitch

Medium Green
Stem Stitch

Medium Rose
Pink
Chain Stitch

Gold Thread
Blanket Stitch

Leaves/
Medium Green
Chain Stitch

Blanket Stitch

Work from the left to the right. Bring the ribbon to the front ¼" from the edge of the felt. Hold the ribbon down with your thumb and make a vertical stitch. Bring the needle over the thread and pull into place. Repeat for the desired length. Make sure the vertical stitches are straight and even.

Japanese Ribbon Stitch

Bring the ribbon to the front. Hold the ribbon flat with a little give (about ⅛") so that the ribbon will not be pulled completely flat. Pierce the ribbon in the center. Gently pull the ribbon to the back so that it curls at the top. Do not pull the ribbon too tight.

Chain Stitch

Bring the ribbon up and hold it down with your thumb. Reinsert the needle and come back up. Be sure the needle comes up over the ribbon to form a loop. Continue to form next loop. Repeat for the desired length. Secure the last loop with a short straight stitch.

Stem Stitch

Work from the left to the right. Bring the needle up and back down. Come up at the center of the previous stitch and go back down above and to the right as shown. Continue to sew along the line for the desired length, keeping the ribbon to the left of the needle.

Straight Stitch

Bring the ribbon to the front and back down to form a simple, flat stitch.

Spider Web Rose

Use sewing thread to make 5 straight stitches of equal length for the base. Bring the ribbon up at the center. Weave the ribbon alternately over and under the spokes of the base to fill, keeping the ribbon loose and allowing it to twist slightly. Secure the ribbon at the back after the last wrap.

Chain Stitch Rose

Start with a small chain stitch for the center of the rose. Continue to work chain stitches in a tight spiral around the center. Make 1 or 2 circles until the rose is the desired size. Secure the last stitch with a small straight stitch.

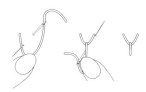

French Knot

Bring the ribbon to the front. Loosely wrap the ribbon around the needle 2 times, keeping the ribbon flat. Reinsert the needle into the fabric very close to where the needle came up. Pull the needle to the back, holding the wraps in place while pulling the ribbon through.

Fly Stitch

Bring the ribbon to the front and back down. Hold the ribbon in a loop and bring the needle back up as shown. Be sure the needle comes up over the ribbon to form a V. Go back down to make a short straight stitch.

Christmassy
Pillow Wraps

**Instructions begin
on page 71.**
Patterns are full size.

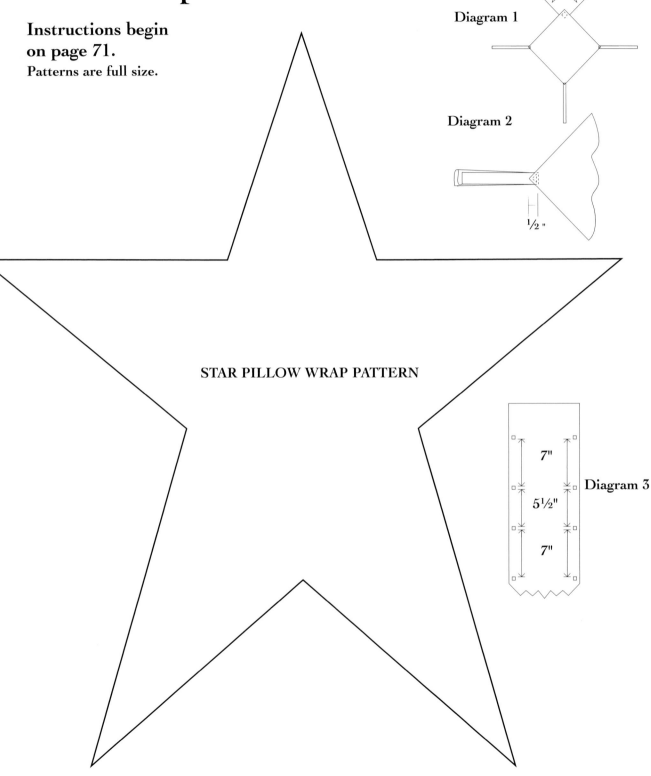

Diagram 1

Diagram 2

½ "

STAR PILLOW WRAP PATTERN

7"

5½"   Diagram 3

7"

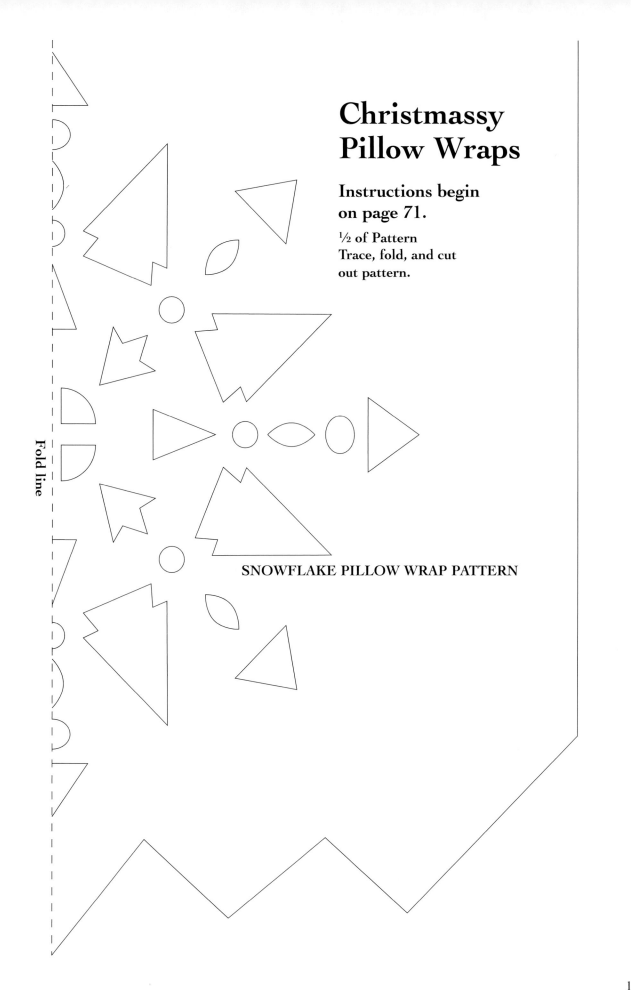

Christmassy Pillow Wraps

Instructions begin on page 71.

½ of Pattern
Trace, fold, and cut
out pattern.

SNOWFLAKE PILLOW WRAP PATTERN

Fold line

Velvet and Organza Stocking

Instructions begin on page 56.

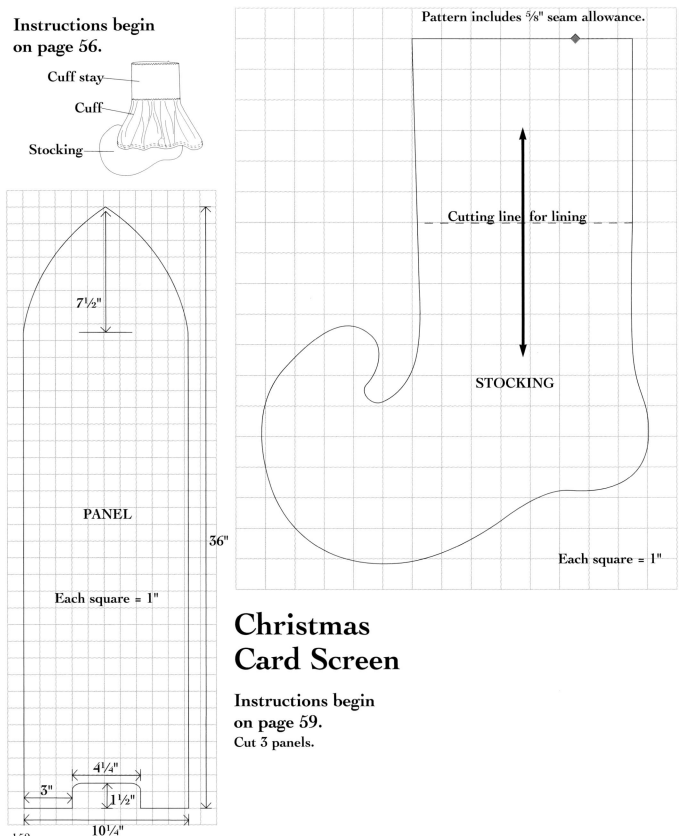

Cuff stay

Cuff

Stocking

Pattern includes ⅝" seam allowance.

_ _ Cutting line for lining _ _ _ _

STOCKING

Each square = 1"

7½"

PANEL

36"

Each square = 1"

4¼"

3"

1½"

10¼"

Christmas Card Screen

Instructions begin on page 59.
Cut 3 panels.

152

Velvet Tree Skirt

Instructions begin on page 27.

Pattern is full size.

POINT PATTERN

Tree Skirt Cutting Diagram

36"

1½"

Cutting lines

Cut on bias.

Jeweled Candle Collars

Instructions begin on page 38.

Patterns are full size.

Cutting Patterns

Large collar

Small collar

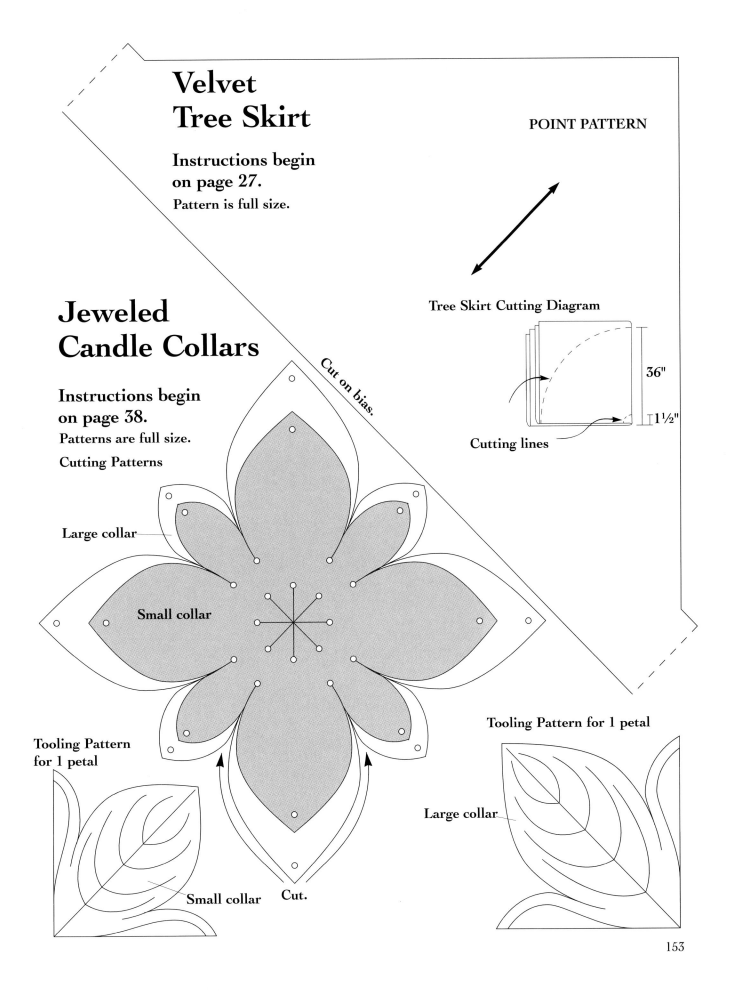

Tooling Pattern for 1 petal

Small collar

Cut.

Tooling Pattern for 1 petal

Large collar

Sources

Page 6—Look for *Donna Hamilton's Gracious Country Inns & Favorite Recipes* at local bookstores or write The Mockingbird Company, 5115 Wetheredsville Rd., Baltimore, MD 21207.

Page 8—Write to The Inn at Blackberry Farm, 1471 West Millers Cove Road, Walland, TN 37886, or call (800) 862-7610.

Page 14—Write to The Inn at Perry Cabin, 308 Watkins Lane, St. Michaels, MD 21663, or call (800) 722-2949.

Page 18—Write to Dairy Hollow House, 515 Spring Street, Eureka Springs, AR 72632, or call (800) 562-8650.

Page 24—cone: For information on stores carrying cone, call Heeney Company, Inc. at (404) 351-0000.

Page 27—velvet: For information on stores carrying Waverly velvet, call (800) 423-5881.

Page 28—beads: For information on stores and mail-order sources carrying The Beadery® Craft Products, call (401) 539-2432.

Pages 30 and 34—Styrofoam ball: Schrock's International, P.O. Box 538, Bolivar, OH 44612. Send $3 for catalog or call (216) 874-3700.

ribbon: For information on stores carrying ribbon, call Heeny

Page 40

Company, Inc. at (404) 351-0000.

Page 38—brass and copper foil: St. Louis Crafts, Inc., 7606 Idaho Avenue, Saint Louis, MO 63111-3219, or call (800) 841-7631.

Page 40—wooden plate: Look for Walnut Hollow Woodcraft products at leading crafts stores, or call (608) 935-2341.

Page 8

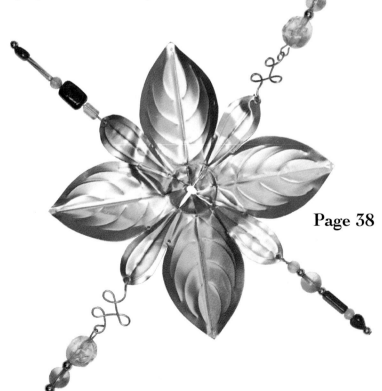

Page 38

paint: Look for DecoArt™ paints at local crafts stores. Or contact DecoArt, P.O. Box 360, Stanford, KY 40484, or call (606) 365-3193.

paintbrushes: Loew-Cornell, Inc., 563 Chestnut Avenue, Teaneck, NJ 07666-2490, or call (201) 836-7070.

Page 44—sweet potato chips: For information on stores carrying Terra Chips®, call (718) 349-7171.

Page 52—German chocolate coffee granules: To order Barnie's coffees, call Barnie's Coffee & Tea Company® at (800) 284-1416.

Page 62

Pages 57 and 58—fabric: For information on stores carrying Waverly fabrics, call (800) 423-5881.

Page 62—craft clay: For information on stores carrying American Art Clay products, call (800) 374-1600.

Page 72—wreath: Laurel Springs Christmas Tree Farm, P.O. Box 85, Laurel Springs, NC

28644-0085, or call (800) 851-2345.

Page 92—candles: Susan Schadt Designs, 2120 Jimmy Durante Boulevard, Suite 108, Del Mar, CA 92014, or call (800) 459-4595.

Page 96—mesh ribbon: For information on stores carrying mesh ribbon, call Heeney Company, Inc. at (404) 351-0000.

Page 98—apron: Williams-Sonoma, 100 North Point Street, San Francisco, CA 94123, or call (415) 616-8647.

Page 100—silk ribbon: YLI Corporation, P.O. Box 109, Provo, UT 84603-0109, or call (801) 377-3900.

felt: Look for Kunin Felt Classic Rainbow™ Felt products at local retail fabric stores, or call (603) 929-6100 for mail-order prices.

Page 104—polar fleece: Thorburn's, 123 Nashua Road, Suite 128, Londonderry, NH 03053, or call (603) 437-4924.

Page 107—napkins: Caspari, 225 5th Avenue, Suite 637, New York, NY 10010, or call (800) CASPARI.

Page 108—fabric: For information on stores carrying Waverly fabrics, call (800) 423-5881.

ribbon: Hymen Hendler & Sons, 67 West 38th Street, New York, NY 10018, or call (212) 840-8393.

Page 112—stamps and paint: Hot Potatoes Fabric Stamps, 209 10th Avenue South, Suite 311, Nashville, TN 37203. Send $3 for catalog or call (615) 255-4055.

burlap: Loose Ends, 3824 River Road North, Keizer, OR 97303, or call (800) 390-9979.

Page 114—stamps and ink: Personal Stamp Exchange, 360 Sutton Place, Santa Rosa, CA 95407, or call (707) 588-8058.

Page 114—crinkle wire: D. Blumchen & Company, Inc., P.O. Box 1210-OX, Ridgewood, NJ 07451-1210, or call (201) 652-5595.

Page 123—corrugated cardboard: Loose Ends, 3824 River Road North, Keizer, OR 97303, or call (800) 390-9979.

Page 140—miniature baskets: Charlotte & Company, 4232 Dolly Ridge Rd., Birmingham, AL 35243, or call (205) 967-3163.

Page 142—pottery: T. Weber Pottery, 1313 4th Avenue North, Nashville, TN 37208, or call (615) 726-6001.

Page 112

General Index

Angel pillow and ornament, 64
Apron, 98

Banner, mailbox, 74
Bath oil and powder, 96
Blackberry Farm, Inn at, 8
Bottle, ribbon-covered, 96
Bottle toppers, 62

Candle collars, 38
Christmas cards and tags, 114
Christmas card screen, 58
Craft clay, bottle toppers, and
    lamp finials, 62

Dairy Hollow House, 18
Decoupage plate and candle-
    sticks, 68

Fabric-wrapped boxes, 108

Garlands, paper bag, 66
Gift bags
    no-sew, 112
    shopping, 110
Gift boxes, fabric-wrapped, 108
Gift cards, 114
Gift wrappings, 106

Holly garlands, 66

Inns
    Dairy Hollow House, 18

Page 60

Inn at Blackberry Farm, 8
Inn at Perry Cabin, 14

Lamp finials, 62

Mailbox banner, 74

Oak leaf wreath, 72
Ornaments
    stenciled angel, 64
    silk ribbon embroidery and
    felt, 100
    wire-and-bead, 28

Painted charger, napkin, and
    tablecloth, 40
Painted tray, 60
Painting
    charger, 40
    napkin, 40
    tablecloth, 40
    tray, 60
Paper bag holly garlands, 66
Paper napkin wraps, 106

Page 62

Perry Cabin, Inn at, 14
Picture mat, 102
Pillows
    stenciled angel, 64
    wraps, 70
Pillow wraps, 70
Place mats, 36
Powder box, ribbon-covered, 96

Scarf and mittens, 104
Seasonal topiaries, 24
Sewing
    apron, 98
    ornaments and pin, 100
    pillow and ornament, 64
    pillow wraps, 70
    place mats, 36
    scarf and mittens, 104
    stocking, 56
    tree skirt, 26
Shopping/gift bags, 110
Silk ribbon embroidered orna-
    ments and pin, 100
Spiced fruit, 54
Stenciling
    charger, 40
    pillow and ornament, 64
    tablecloth, 40
Stocking, 56

Topiaries
    seasonal, 24
    velvet, 34
Tray, painted, 60
Tree skirt, 26
Tree topper, 30

Velvet topiaries, 34

Wire-and-bead ornaments, 28
Wreath, oak leaf, 72

Page 72

Recipe Index

Page 129

Almonds
  Pepper Nuts, 120
  Tart, Rustic Almond-Pear, 127
Appetizers
  Cheese
      Bites, Ham and Cheese
        Potato, 45
      Savory Cocktail Tree, 93
      Terrine, Italian Cheese, 123
  Cranberry Tapenade, 44
  Fritters, Confetti, 122
  Gorp, Sugar and Spice, 120
  Nuts, Pepper, 120
  Pecans, Brown Sugar-
    Cinnamon, 50
  Sausage Quiches,
    Sourdough-, 45
  Turkey Sandwiches, Mini, 45

Beans with Country Ham,
  Green, 139
Beverages
  Coffee, Frosted, 53
  Eggnog, Iced, 47
Breads. *See also* Cornbreads.
  Rolls, Rum-Glazed Coffee, 53
  Scones, 17
  Terra-Cotta Table Bread, 90
  Yeast
      Sally Lunn French
        Toast, 12
Butter
  Cake, Butter-Pecan, 143
  Frosting, Butter-Pecan, 143
  Honey-Pecan Butter, 13
  Pie, Browned Butter Pecan, 21
  Sage Butter, Mashed Potatoes
    with, 138

Cakes. *See also* Cookies.
  Butter-Pecan Cake, 143
  Cheesecake, Frozen
    Pistachio, 129
  Chocolate-Amaretto Cake,
    Dark, 78
  Fruitcake, White Chocolate
    Chunk, 126
  Peanutty Layer Cake, 130

Candies
  Bonbons, Lemon
    Cream, 118
  Truffles, German Chocolate, 52
  White Chocolate Star
    Package, 88
Caramel
  Brownies, Caramel-
    Walnut, 80
  Logs, Frozen Toffee, 82
  Sauce, Quick Caramel, 127
Carrots, Sage-Roasted Turkey
  with Glazed, 138
Casseroles
  Oyster and Onion au
    Gratin, 139
Cheese. *See also* Appetizers/
  Cheese.
  au Gratin, Oyster and
    Onion, 139
Cheesecake, Frozen
  Pistachio, 129
Chocolate
  Bars and Cookies
      Brownies, Caramel-
        Walnut, 80
      Chewies, Easy
        Chocolate, 85

Cakes and Tortes
  Amaretto Cake, Dark
    Chocolate-, 78
  Fruitcake, White Chocolate
    Chunk, 126
  Mint Torte, Chocolate, 78
Candies
  Truffles, German
    Chocolate, 52
  White Chocolate Star
    Package, 88
Pie, Walnut Fudge, 132
Sauces
    Fudge Sauce,
      Heavenly, 132
    Mocha Fondue, 51
  Trifle, Peanut Butter
    Brownie, 85
Coconut Frosting,
  Peanut-, 130
Coffee
  Bars, Coffee, 52
  Cookies, Slice 'n' Bake
    Coffee, 51
  Frosted Coffee, 53
  Pie, Coffee Crunch, 81
  Rolls, Rum-Glazed
    Coffee, 53

Cookies
  Bars and Squares
      Caramel-Walnut
         Brownies, 80
      Coffee Bars, 52
   Biscotti, Pumpkin Pie, 46
   Chocolate Chewies,
      Easy, 85
   Rolled
      Coffee Cookies, Slice 'n'
         Bake, 51
      Sugar Cookie Christmas
         Ornaments, 121
   Sandwich Cookies,
      Snowball, 118
   Sugar Cookie Ice Cream
      Sandwiches, 83
Cornbreads
   Country Christmas
      Cornbread, 122
   Fritters, Confetti, 122
   Mix , Sundance Cornmeal, 122
   Skillet-Sizzled Buttermilk
      Cornbread, 21
   Strata, Crescent's Overnight
      Cornbread, 21
Cranberries
   Dressing, Cranberry-
      Walnut, 138
   Salad, Frozen Cranberry-
      Gingersnap, 140
   Tapenade, Cranberry, 44
Custard, French Toast, 13

Desserts. See also Cakes, Cookies,
   Pies and Pastries.
   Bombe, Bourbon-Pecan
      Macaroon, 127
   Chocolate
      Peanut Butter Brownie
         Trifle, 85
      Torte, Chocolate Mint, 78
   Frozen
      Toffee Logs, Frozen, 82
   Sauces
      Caramel Sauce, Quick, 127
      Fondue, Mocha, 51
      Fudge Sauce,
         Heavenly, 132
   Dressing, Cranberry-
      Walnut, 138

Eggnog, Iced, 47

Fillings. See Frostings.
French Toast, Sally Lunn, 12
Frostings, Fillings, and Toppings
   Butter-Pecan Frosting, 143
   Fruits, Warm Winter, 13
   Peanut-Coconut Frosting, 130
   Preserves, Raspberry, 17
Fruit. See also specific types.
   Warm Winter Fruits, 13

Ham
   Bites, Ham and Cheese
      Potato, 45
   Green Beans with Country
      Ham, 139
   Strata, Crescent's Overnight
      Cornbread, 21
Honey-Pecan Butter, 13

Ice Cream Sandwiches, Sugar
   Cookie, 83

Lemon Cream Bonbons, 118

Olives
   Tree, Savory Cocktail, 93
Oyster and Onion au Gratin, 139

Peanut Butter Brownie Trifle, 85
Peanuts
   Cake, Peanutty Layer, 130
   Frosting, Peanut-Coconut, 130
   Gorp, Sugar and Spice, 120
Pear Tart, Rustic Almond-, 127
Pecans
   Bombe, Bourbon-Pecan
      Macaroon, 127
   Brown Sugar-Cinnamon
      Pecans, 50
   Butter, Honey-Pecan, 13
   Cake, Butter-Pecan, 143
   Frosting, Butter-Pecan, 143
   Pie, Browned Butter
      Pecan, 21
   Tartlets, Maple-Pecan, 46
Pies and Pastries
   Butternut Spice Pie, 140
   Coffee Crunch Pie, 81
   Fudge Pie, Walnut, 132

Hazelnut Buttercrunch
   Pie, 133
Macadamia Pie, 126
Pecan Pie, Browned
   Butter, 21
Shells, Cinnamon Pastry, 47
Tarts
   Almond-Pear Tart,
      Rustic, 127
   Maple-Pecan Tartlets, 46
Potatoes
   Bites, Ham and Cheese
      Potato, 45
   Mashed Potatoes with Sage
      Butter, 138
Preserves, Raspberry, 17
Pumpkin Pie Biscotti, 46

Quiches, Sourdough-
   Sausage, 45

Raspberry Preserves, 17
Relishes
   Cranberry Tapenade, 44
Rolls. See Breads.

Salad, Frozen Cranberry-
   Gingersnap, 140
Salami
   Terrine, Italian Cheese, 123
Sandwiches, Mini
   Turkey, 45
Sauces. See Desserts/Sauces.
Sausage Quiches,
   Sourdough-, 45
Squash
   Butternut Spice Pie, 140
Stuffing. See Dressing.
Syrup, Cinnamon-Maple, 13

Turkey
   Sage-Roasted Turkey with
      Glazed Carrots, 138
   Sandwiches, Mini Turkey, 45

Walnuts
   Brownies, Caramel-
      Walnut, 80
   Dressing, Cranberry-
      Walnut, 138
   Pie, Walnut Fudge, 132

Contributors

Designers

Heidi Borchers, paper bag holly garlands, 66–67.

Janice Cox, bath oil and powder, 96–97.

Charlotte Hagood, candle collars, 38–39; spiced fruit, 54–55; oak leaf wreath, 72–73; bottle and powder box, 96–97.

Susan Harrison, original art, 102–103.

Deborah Hastings, Christmas card screen, 58–59.

Linda Hendrickson, pillow wraps, 70–71.

Margot Hotchkiss, velvet topiaries, 34–35; place mats, 36–37; angel pillow and ornament, 64–65; decoupage plate and candlesticks, 68–69; shopping/gift bags, 110–111; Christmas cards and tags, 114–115.

Heidi Tyline King, tree skirt, 26–27.

Julie McGuffee, silk ribbon ornaments and pin, 100–101.

Duffy Morrison, stocking, 56–57; apron, 98–99; fabric-wrapped boxes, 108–109.

Cathy Muir, wire-and-bead ornaments, 28–29; painted tray, 60–61.

Mary O'Neil, Hot Potatoes Fabric Stamps, no-sew gift bags, 112–113.

Dondra Parham, tree topper, 30–31.

Carole Sullivan, seasonal topiaries, 24–25.

Elizabeth Taliaferro, recipes and packaging, 116–123.

Carol Tipton, painted tableware, 40–41.

Patricia Weaver, napkin-wrapped boxes, 106–107.

Cyndi Wheeler, scarf and mittens, 104–105.

Claudia Williams, bottle toppers and lamp finials, 62–63.

Photographers

Jim Bathie, front cover, 2, 4–5, 6, left and right; 7–13, 18–21, 42–54, 76–93, 116–143, 154, left; 158.

Gary Clark, 22–25.

Keith Harrelson, 26–27, 66–67, 106–107, 112–113.

Chuck King, 41.

Larry Martin, 6, center; 14–17.

Lisa Masson, 71.

John O'Hagan, back cover, 3, 28–41, 56–65, 68–75, 94–105, 108–111, 114–115, 154, right; 155–157.

David Thomason, 100.

Photo Stylists

Kay Clarke, front cover, 2, 4–5, 6, left and right; 7–13, 18–21, 42–54, 76–93, 116–143, 154, left; 158.

Katie Stoddard, back cover, 3, 22–41, 56–75, 94–115, 154, right; 155–157.

Acknowledgments

Thanks to the following people:
Blake Brinson
Stephen Creese
Ginny Izydore

Thanks to the following homeowners:
Jane and John George
Val and George Holman
Loretta and Bill Morton
Michaele and Morris Padgett
Dolly and James Walker
Linda and Kneeland Wright

Thanks to the following businesses:
Ann Gish,
Newbury Park, California
Bridges Antiques,
Birmingham, Alabama
Bromberg & Co., Inc.,
Birmingham, Alabama
Charlotte & Company,
Birmingham, Alabama
Dorothy McDaniel's Flowers,
Birmingham, Alabama
Frankie Engel Antiques,
Birmingham, Alabama
The Holly Tree, Inc.,
Birmingham, Alabama
Lace-n-Stone,
Santa Cruz, California
Lamb's Ears Ltd.,
Birmingham, Alabama
Paul Ecke Ranch,
Encinitas, California
Waverly,
New York, New York

CHRISTMAS CARD LIST

Name & Address	Sent	Name & Address	Sent